Pupils as Playwrights

drama, literacy and playwriting

Pupils as Playwrights
drama, literacy and playwriting

Brian Woolland

Trentham Books
Stoke on Trent, UK and Sterling, USA

KH

Trentham Books Limited

Westview House   22883 Quicksilver Drive
734 London Road   Sterling
Oakhill   VA 20166-2012
Stoke on Trent   USA
Staffordshire
England ST4 5NP

First published 2008

British Library Cataloguing-in-Publication Data
A catalogue record for this book is available from the British Library

ISBN: 978 1 85856 427 2

Designed and typeset by Trentham Print Design Ltd, Chester and printed in Great Britain by Page Bros (Norwich) Ltd.

2/9/10

CONTENTS

Acknowledgements • vii

SECTION ONE

Introduction • 1

Dramatic Writing and Process Drama • 9

SECTION TWO: PLAY(FUL) WRITING • 15

Dialogue and voice • 17

Character and role • 27

Structure, story and narrative • 35

Meanings beyond the literal • 49

Observation • 55

SECTION THREE: PRACTICAL PROJECTS • 63

Years 1 and 2
Jack and the Beanstalk • 65
Not Now Bernard • 73

Years 2 and 3
The Pet Cellar • 77
Voices in the Park • 85

Years 3 and 4
The Kraken • 91

Years 4 and 5
Wolves in the Walls • 105

Years 5, 6 and above
The Dunce (Le cancre) • 111

Year 6 and above
The Arrival • 127
The Fall of Troy • 153

Glossary of drama techniques • 173

SECTION FOUR: RESOURCES • 177

Photocopiable materials • 179

Online resources and internet links • 195

Bibliography • 197

Index • 199

ACKNOWLEDGEMENTS

I would like to thank all those who have contributed directly or indirectly to this book, in particular the children, young people, students and teachers who have made such active contributions to the development of much of this material in classes and work-shops.

Thanks also to Trentham Books and to Gillian Klein for commissioning this title and for her advice and support during the writing.

To Liz Taylor at Liverpool John Moore's University.

To Mrs Rothwell, Headteacher, and the children of William Gladstone C.E Primary School, Seaforth, Liverpool, some of whose work is used on the cover.

To John Fines, who, without knowing it, set the ball rolling.

To Hilary, for her support and for the inspiration of her own work with children.

The Dunce is a translation of *Le cancre* by Jacques Prévert, first published in *Paroles*. Copyright: (c) **Editions Gallimard, Paris, 1949**. Reproduced by permission of Editions Gallimard.

National Curriculum documentation and extracts from the *Primary Framework for literacy and mathematics* is Crown Copyright material and is reproduced with the permission of the Controller of HMSO and the Queen's Printer for Scotland.

Permissions disclaimer to be added

A note about the front cover

The paintings and drawings reproduced on the front cover are by primary school children who had been asked to draw what might be reflected in their eyes as they looked out at the world around them.

SECTION ONE

Introduction

'One can play wisely with a doll or play foolishly at chess.' Janusz Korczak

'Good learning is always active learning, in which the children, rather than the teacher, do the work ... Active learning leads to understanding.' John Fines (1994: 125)

About the book

This is a book about drama, literacy and play; a book about playing with language; about making the development of language and the acquisition of literacy skills a joyous and playful experience. It has been developed out of numerous workshops and classes with children and teachers – in schools and universities, on continuous professional development (CPD) days and courses.

It is mainly for teachers working in Primary Schools and for students training to work in schools but it should also be useful for anyone working with young people between the ages of 6 and 13. This age range deliberately transcends school barriers in the English state educational system. In other English speaking countries the age of transfer between Primary and Secondary ranges between 11 and 13. The book is written for teachers who would like to use drama in the development of all forms of literacy. It assumes a basic knowledge of educational drama on the part of the reader but not great experience or expertise. And it offers ways of working that associate the development of literacy skills very closely with the development of speaking and listening skills.

The title

Pupils   The word *pupil* has two discrete meanings: 'one who is taught' *or* 'the circular opening of an eye, through which light passes to the retina'. The pun is intentional. Playwrights are observers of the world around them.

as The word refers to role play; children behaving as if they were playwrights, adopting some of the attitudes of mind of a playwright.

playwrights The Collins English Dictionary gives the definition of a 'wright' as 'a person who creates, builds or repairs something specified: a playwright, shipwright.' The playwright is a maker of plays, just as a shipwright is a maker of ships. But the phrase 'play writing' also contains an apposite pun. Children who engage in the playful writing proposed in this book will not only be writing plays. One of my key aims is to enable and encourage children to play with writing, for their writing to become a playful, exploratory activity; in which they can explore different voices and registers, tones and rhythms through writing, in much the same way that they might experiment with different roles and attitudes in drama.

The book argues that many of the skills developed by playwrights can be learnt, and are very valuable in developing literacy in children.

The book offers

- ◼ a rationale and a methodology for introducing dramatic writing of various kinds into the curriculum for young people from the ages of 6 to 13

- ◼ suggestions for practical work in the form of tasks, exercises, activities and extended practical projects, including accounts of and suggestions for sustained process drama

- ◼ discussion of the ideas and theories underpinning that practical work

- ◼ a range of examples of good practice, providing teachers with materials with which they can encourage and enable children:

  - – to play with language, to explore meaning and relationships between the spoken and written word

  - – to play with metaphor, with dialogue and voice, with register and tone

  - – to play with structure, narrative and story

  - – to develop observational skills

–   to approach their reading in a spirit of enquiry, developing the skills which make for active, speculative and reflective readers

–   to create effective and affecting writing

■   some photocopiable material for use with children, together with advice on how to develop similar materials.

It does not aim to teach children how to become playwrights, although if some do go on to write plays, hopefully they will do so because they are curious about people, about the ways we interact with each other and our social environment, excited by the richness of language and the strangely revealing ways people use it.

Creativity, drama and literacy

After several years in which drama and other arts subjects have been sidelined in schools, there has recently been growing recognition of the importance of creativity and of drama in particular. Although at the time of writing the National Curriculum for England, as published in 1999 and still in force, has itself not been updated, the Qualifications and Curriculum Authority (QCA) has published documentation specifically designed to promote creativity in teaching and learning across the curriculum (see Resources, Section Four). Under the heading *'Why is creativity so important?'*, the documentation suggests that

When pupils are thinking and behaving creatively in the classroom, you are likely to see them:

■   questioning and challenging

■   making connections and seeing relationships

■   envisaging what might be

■   exploring ideas, keeping options open

■   reflecting critically on ideas, actions and outcomes.

The *Creativity* documentation recognises, above all, that 'Creative pupils lead richer lives and, in the longer term, make a valuable contribution to society'. The recently revised Primary Framework for literacy and mathematics also recognises the importance of creativity and acknowledges that the kind of cross-curricular work so central to good process drama is very valuable: 'Making links between curriculum subjects and areas of learning deepens children's understanding by providing opportunities to reinforce and en-hance learning.'

Paulo Freire in his seminal work *Pedagogy of the Oppressed* distinguishes be-tween what he termed 'banking' educational systems and a 'problem-posing' educational approach. In the 'bank' model, students are treated as objects, filled with knowledge, to an agenda chosen by expert teachers; in the 'problem-posing' model, students are subjects, developing 'their own power to perceive critically the way they exist in the world with which and in which they find themselves' (Freire, 1970:64). Problem-posing education affirms children 'as beings in the process of becoming' (Freire, 1970:65).

What the recently published QCA documentation about creativity appears not to recognise is that there are inherent contradictions between the belated championing of creativity and the restrictive 'bank' model of the National Curriculum itself. Whilst this book cannot attempt to resolve those contra-dictions – and it may well be that the Curriculum itself is changed to address the issue – there is no doubt in my mind that the pupils of my title are children who are given opportunities to see the world through their own eyes, whose insights are valued and who learn through their playful interaction with the social world. Learning to be literate involves negotiating meanings with others. It must involve playing with language, trying out language, exploring connections between spoken and written words, exploring meaning, and how meaning is generated.

Drama in schools

Drama is an art form in which we can explore relationships between our selves and our social and cultural environments; it is specifically and essen-tially both social and collaborative. In school, drama activities range from children's structured play, through small classroom improvisations and group work to sustained process drama and public performances. It is not within the scope of this book to argue the value, the power and the potential of drama in education – many others have done that.

The approach now known as process drama is difficult to define because it is a fluid form, though it can be characterised as being likely to include the following features:

- ■ an overarching dramatic fiction provides a unifying aesthetic, social and pedagogical context for a drama which develops over an ex-tended period of time

- the developing dramatic fiction gives coherence to a range of activities

- these activities draw on a wide range of dramatic forms and work in different curriculum areas

- students take on roles within the drama, enabling them to explore and experiment with a range of attitudes, opinions, points of view and voices

- outcomes of these explorations are not predetermined

- there is an emphasis on exploration by the participants rather than performance for those outside it

- the teacher (or leader) sometimes works within the dramatic fiction, taking a role, sometimes outside it, setting tasks, reflecting on decisions made and helping to tease out meanings created within the drama

- the process is essentially collaborative, epitomising Freire's model of 'problem-posing education'.

Process drama is undoubtedly a rich and rewarding way of working for children and for teachers. Time and again I have seen children in all manner of educational contexts working in process dramas at levels way beyond what might normally be expected of them. Process drama exemplifies the concept of the 'zone of proximal development' formulated by the developmental psychologist, L S Vygotsky:

> The distance between a child's actual developmental level as determined by independent problem solving and the higher level of potential development as determined through problem solving under adult guidance or in collaboration with more capable peers. (Vygotsky, 1978)

In process drama the collaboration of teacher and children provides a dual 'scaffold' for learning, enabling children to contribute in and out of role and to learn from the contributions of others (teacher and peers) within and in response to the developing fiction.

Playwriting and process drama

Where then might playwriting fit into this pedagogical model? If playwriting means an individual working alone to produce a play for performance by others, then it probably doesn't. This book, however, argues that playwriting can be seen as an extension of writing in role, writing which arises out of a dramatic fiction and feeds back into it, encouraging active reflection. It is not a big jump to move from writing in role (adopting an appropriate voice, tone, register and vocabulary) to writing dialogue, assigning words to people. Seen like this, playwriting becomes not just an extension of writing in role but a way of exploring relationships between the spoken and the written word. The playwriting tasks, exercises and activities suggested here are designed to give children opportunities to write in the way that they hear language used, and then to listen to their own words in use. This process itself is immensely valuable, and the focus of the playwriting proposed in this book is as much on the craft of the playwright, and how this relates to what children can achieve in their writing, as on what might be produced as a result. The range of skills and activities that a playwright practices, develops and refines includes:

- close observation of human behaviour in social contexts

- writing in various voices

- selecting and using appropriate vocabulary, register, tone and rhythm

- editing

- structuring and shaping

- communicating character, narrative and situation through dialogue

- reflecting on meaning

The plays that children might write using the methods proposed in this book could be as short as six lines, as pithy as Japanese haiku. The work is liberating and empowering: liberating from the restraints of poor self-esteem; empowering because it enables the child to explore voices and attitudes other than their own, to experience the power of observing the effect of their writing on others. The playwriting tasks, exercises and activities can all be used in a self-contained way, valuable tools in their own right for developing literacy; they can complement process drama work; or they can be integrated into it. And process drama can itself be seen as a kind of collaborative play making – not necessarily resulting in a play to be performed to an external audience, but one in which the participants are active throughout as both makers and readers of their own work.

Organisation of the book

Dramatic Writing and Process Drama discusses the richness of exploratory process drama, looking at a range of ways in which writing in role, reading in role and some of the playwriting tasks and exercises suggested in Section Two, can be incorporated and integrated into process drama, enhancing and enriching the drama whilst developing literacy.

Section Two, *Play(ful) Writing*, focuses on key elements of play writing which are highly relevant both to the development of literacy skills and to children's abilities to work meaningfully in drama. Each chapter starts with a discussion of the thinking that underpins it. This is followed by suggestions for practical work, usually in the form of a range of tasks and exercises and how they might be developed. The ideas introduced in these chapters are relevant to children of all ages, although they will demand different practical approaches and are likely to be introduced in different ways, depending on the age and the abilities of the children. Most of the tasks and exercises can be used with a whole class, with small groups or with individuals. They do not demand extended drama time or specialised drama space. Used in this way, they might complement other work on literacy as well as enhancing drama work, including process drama. Each chapter in this section also includes a discussion of the ways in which some of the tasks can be integrated into process drama.

Section Three of the book contains a series of nine *Practical Projects*, each demonstrating how the ideas and the material in Section Two might be used in practice with different age groups. These projects include a wide range of work and approaches. All highlight issues of literacy and include suggestions for further work. Although most of the work described in these projects has been developed and used with real classes of real children, they are suggestions for practice, not prescriptions. For this reason, I have not presented them in the form of schemes of work with lesson plans. Although each of the projects is designed for a specific age group, you will find that much of the material is readily adaptable for use with other ages.

The practical projects are followed by a *Glossary of Drama Techniques*. This is far from exhaustive, only referring to techniques suggested in the projects themselves. It is intended as a reference point, a kind of shorthand. I offer this with some hesitation. These techniques are sometimes referred to as Drama Conventions or Drama Strategies. As David Davis (2005:164-5) has argued, the danger is that they are taken out of context and used as ends in themselves, leading to a wholly pragmatic, bits and pieces approach to drama. In this instance, however, I hope that situating examples within the context of the projects shows how the techniques can be used and why they are useful.

Section Four, *Resources*, includes photocopiable teaching material, recommendations for further reading, online resources and internet links, guidance as to where to find further material, and a bibliography.

How to use the book

Many of the tasks, exercises and activities proposed in this book can be used in self-contained ways or appropriated and adapted for use as part of more general literacy work. They can also be integrated into larger dramatic fictions, becoming part of sustained process drama; and that, in ideal circumstances, is how I see the book being most valuable. Although the focus of the book is not on process drama, all the suggestions are intended to complement and enrich such work.

Given the pressures of delivering a prescriptive curriculum, many teachers are unable to devote as much time as they would like to working in drama. The work proposed in this book can therefore be used as part of extended projects, to initiate them, to deepen and/or consolidate other work; or as relatively self-contained exercises that are beneficial in their own right. But in all the work, even in some of the more structured exercises, my concern is to focus on the needs and the interests of the child, and to find ways of working which enable children to explore content and experiment with dramatic form at the same time as they play with spoken and written language.

The book is extensively cross-referenced. Although there is a clear progression in the ordering of chapters, it is organised to enable you to use material from Sections Two or Three as it suits your needs and the needs of the children you're working with. For the beginner, I hope you will find ideas that you can try out immediately. For the more experienced practitioner, I would hope that, as you become familiar with the ideas and the approach, you experiment and develop your own materials and projects; and that the work you undertake with the children in your classes is as enriching for you as it is for them.

Use of the personal pronoun

I recognise that there are many excellent male teachers in Primary Schools; they are in a minority. I therefore refer throughout to the teacher as 'she', except in *The Kraken* project, where I am the teacher referred to!

Dramatic Writing and Process Drama

> Process drama is almost synonymous with the term drama in education. The phrase process drama seems to have arisen ... in the late 1980s as an attempt to distinguish this particular dramatic approach from less complex and ambitious improvised activities and to locate it in a wider dramatic and theatrical context ... The practices of drama in education and, by extension process drama, are increasingly recognised as radical and coherent theatrical experiences. They challenge traditional notions of the creation and function of character and narrative, as well as of a traditional spectator-performer relationship... Brad Haseman notes that those working in process drama have created, appropriated, and reshaped a range of dramatic forms that establish its unique character. For Haseman, these forms include role taking and role building, the 'key strategy' of teacher-in-role, the means of being inside and outside the action, and distance and reflection. (O'Neill, 1995, xv, xvii-xviii)

In the introduction I proposed that process drama can itself be seen as a kind of collaborative play making, in which the participants effectively take on the roles of playwright, director, actor and, crucially, audience. There are two important qualifications to this assertion. The first, that the play will not necessarily proceed in a linear fashion:

> ... It is important not to allow the linear development of story-line to take over. If it happens, the work may become merely a series of incidents – 'what happens next'. Instead, drama is likely to arise from moments of tension and decision ... when (they) ... face the consequences of their actions. (O'Neill and Lambert, 1982:41)

The episodes in a process drama should certainly be linked, but not necessarily in a linear way. The exploration of a situation is driven through the needs to engage the participants, stimulating a thirst for understanding, to create depth and to protect them from their own emotional vulnerabilities. This may well result in a drama which, in retrospect, might appear to have the structure of a montage. The last two projects in Section Three, *The Arrival* and *The Fall of Troy* both have the kind of structural patterns which are charac-

9

teristic of process drama. The opening episode of *The Fall of Troy* focuses on the image of a dead soldier on the beach at Troy; the next is a detailed exploration of the man's life (thus moving back in time). The participants take on the roles of soldiers in the besieging Greek army, then shift to reflect on the experiences of those soldiers. The montage structure evolves so that each episode is engaging in itself, but sheds light on others.

The second important qualification to the idea that process drama is a kind of collaborative playwriting is that the play is not performed to an outside audience – at least during the development of the drama. It may well, however, include elements of performance, as in most of the examples in Section Three. These might include:

- presentations of plans that have been practiced – as in *The Kraken*
- interviews – *Jack and the Beanstalk, The Pet Cellar, The Arrival*
- overheard dialogue – *The Dunce*
- enactment of poem or story as video evidence – *The Dunce*
- presentations of investigations – *The Arrival*
- museum performances, videos or audio recordings – *The Arrival*

Presenting these within the unifying context of the dramatic fiction enables those watching the presentations to read and respond in role. In practice this means that the comments are more likely to be about meaning and interpretation. Thus the teacher can respond to a hesitant group by asking, 'I wonder why nobody will say where they think Jack has gone?'

The participants in process drama can also function as audience through a kind of time slippage. Assuming that everyone has taken part in a particular episode, the teacher may then step out of role and ask the children to reflect on what has happened. Thus in *The Kraken*, the teacher takes on the role of a stranger arriving in a village seeking shelter. Soon afterwards he comes out of role and asks, 'I wonder what the villagers thought about the carpenter?' The children take part in the dramatic interaction, and are then given opportunities to view the episode as if they were outsiders to the action.

The teacher in a process drama is, like the children, both participant and audience; as participant taking a role or roles in the drama, but also guiding it, crucially also functioning as playwright and director, structuring, focusing, slowing things down to explore moments in greater depth, ensuring periods of reflection

Augusto Boal coined the term 'spectactor' to describe the function of the participant in *Forum Theatre*, someone who is both actor and spectator. The term can also usefully be applied to participants in process drama – providing that the actor is seen not necessarily as a performer but as someone who is active.

Participants function in many different ways in a process drama. There are times, such as in *The Kraken* project, where each child takes on a role, in a fictional community – eg the miller, the baker, the farmer. These however, are not characters as they might be in a piece of theatre; their roles are more like areas of responsibility. Pedagogically, the roles give the children a stake in the world of the drama. There are other times, such as in some of the later episodes in *The Arrival* and *The Fall of Troy*, where the participants function more like a Chorus in classical Greek drama, offering a collective voice, but a collective in which the individual voice can be honoured and dissent from the collective can itself be dramatised.

Writing in role

The developing fiction of a process drama necessarily demands a range of different kinds of work from the participants. There are times when they will improvise in small groups, or meet as a whole group to discuss an issue in role; but process drama draws on and feeds into the whole curriculum, stimulating and motivating research. Much of this related work will be writing in role of one kind or another. This can range from emergent writing to sophisticated petitions in which the wording is chosen to reflect a particular register. Above all it gives a context and a purpose to writing. To summarise, it can provide opportunities for children to:

- write under the protective shield of a role
- write for a specific (albeit imagined) reader
- write in different voices
- experiment with vocabulary, speech patterns, rhythm and vocabulary, language tones and registers
- write for purpose
- Write to effect change.

Writing in role is likely to be most effective and most empowering for children when the need for it arises from *within the fiction of the drama*, when situations demand a letter or a text or a document to be created. Writing in role might include:

- advertisements
- census returns
- CVs
- diagrams
- diaries
- directions
- documents
- drawings
- instructions
- interviews
- inventories
- journals
- labels and signs
- letters
- lists
- maps
- memoranda
- messages in code
- newspaper reports, headlines
- posters
- tickets

Examples of all of these can be found in the projects in Section Three.

In my own career as a teacher of drama there have been many practitioners whose work has influenced and changed my own practice in the most positive of ways: Dorothy Heathcote, Gavin Bolton, David Davis and Cecily O'Neill have all been as inspirational as they have been challenging. The person who opened my eyes to the powerful possibilities of writing in role was John Fines (1938-1999), a wonderful teacher and historian who strongly advocated the use of drama in teaching history in schools. I was privileged to observe him working with children on several occasions. One of these was a day spent with a class of Year 5 children on the story of Boudicca (formerly known as Boadicea) queen of the Iceni tribe of East Anglia who led an uprising of the tribes against the occupying forces of the Roman Empire. The morning's work was focused on a question which deeply puzzled him as an historian: how did Boudicca unite tribes who had been at war with each other for many years? The children's ultimate task was collectively to write the speech which she made to the gathered tribal leaders.

I mention this here not simply out of respect to a man whose work 'illuminated all that it touched' (Nichol, 2002:3), but because that morning's work sowed a seed that has grown into this book, demonstrating to me that respecting the children and entrusting them with the challenge of a genuine question enabled them to produce work which was as enlightening to John and me as it was to the children. This was writing in role at its most effective. It is also the model for the speech writing activities in *The Arrival* and *The Fall of Troy*.

Reading in role

Teachers are well aware of the need to value children's work. But whilst it's appropriate to display artwork on the classroom wall, is that the best way to value something that has been written in role? Having asked children to write in role, we should consider *how we might respond in role*; how the writing that they have produced can be *valued within the dramatic fiction*. This enables the child to see their writing having an effect; and can also move the drama forward. That was another of the revelations of John Fines' work on the Boudicca project. Collectively, the class wrote the speech. Then it had to be tested in a dramatic context. Would it work?

Integrating written work into the developing drama not only gives children the excitement of seeing their writing having an effect, but also enhances the drama. Later, it might be appropriate for work to be displayed in the classroom, but in the first instance, we should be concerned as teachers not only to honour and respect the work that children produce, but also to give it significance on its own terms.

Mantle of the Expert

The Mantle of the Expert is a dramatic inquiry based approach to teaching and learning developed by Dorothy Heathcote in the 1980s. Heathcote's work was inspirational in the development of process drama, and is often associated with Mantle of the Expert, although the two are not synonymous. The central idea is that participants take on the collective role of experts in a given field of inquiry, or 'enterprise', as Heathcote now terms it. They might be archaeologists excavating the newly discovered tomb of King Priam of Troy, curators in a Museum of Immigration or naturalists charged with the task of releasing caged animals back into the wild. They are being asked to agree, for the duration of the project, to imagine themselves as that group of archaeologists, curators or naturalists, with jobs and responsibilities.

The approach demands respect for the participants, seeks to honour their work, thereby creating opportunities for them to develop responsibilities within it. But equally it expects participants to take their responsibilities seriously. Mantle of the Expert makes considerable demands on participants. We cannot magically endow children with expertise. What we can do is to give them responsibilities within the drama, interact with them as if they had the expertise, listen to them, be advised by them, and crucially allow them time to build up their own sense of responsibility within the world of the project.

Teaching in role

Teaching in role is central to process drama and Mantle of the Expert work. The different functions of the teacher in role and the different kinds of role that a teacher can take in a process drama are discussed towards the end of the chapter, *Character and Role*.

Tasks and exercises in process drama

Given that Section Two of this book is devoted to tasks, exercises and activities, it might be surprising that I wholeheartedly endorse Cecily O'Neill's assertion:

> When drama techniques are valued only for their capacity to promote specific competencies and achieve precise ends, and remain brief, fragmented, and tightly controlled by the teacher or director, the work is likely to fall far short of the kind of generative dramatic encounter available in process drama. (O'Neill, 1995:5)

Over the years I have taken part in many playwriting workshops, sometimes as a student, sometimes as a workshop leader. I have always found them valuable and often exhilarating. I offer the material in the next section of the book not as an alternative to process drama, but to complement it.

SECTION TWO

Play(ful) Writing

Each of the chapters in this section of the book offers

- a short introduction to the topic

- suggestions for practical work in the form of tasks, exercises and activities, most of which can be used in their own right to develop playwriting skills and literacy

- discussion of how the practical work can be adapted for use in process drama.

Dialogue and voice

The language of drama is not confined to the spoken or written word. It is an interaction of different modes of communication. Facial expression, gestures, body language and spatial relations are all as important in drama as they are in theatre; dialogue can as easily be non-verbal as it can be verbal. This chapter, however, is focused on spoken dialogue.

In courses about playwriting, dialogue is sometimes considered to be the thing that comes last in the making of a play. In his excellent book, *Playwriting a Practical Guide*, Noël Greig advises, 'Character, situation and story generally come before full dialogue is developed ... Get the story idea, explore what happens to who, then show it through what is spoken.' (Greig, 2005:32) When developing process drama we usually start with the situation, a problem that has to be solved; initially at least, the children take on rather generalised roles. They are asked to adopt attitudes rather than pretend to be characters. If there are characters in the drama, they tend to come later. The teacher may take on a role, asking the children to help construct that character – partly by asking how that person might speak. The situation, the context, the roles, the characters, are all developed through the drama. Writing in role can create opportunities for children to think about and explore language used in these situations – both formally and informally.

Greig is, however, careful to qualify his claim with that word 'generally'. There are no hard and fast rules for learning the craft of playwriting. Some playwrights start with dialogue, then ask themselves the questions, 'Who is talking? What is the situation and what's the story?' That is an approach I favour – particularly in schools – because it is something that is immediately accessible to children, because children play with dialogue and voice from a very young age. They enjoy putting on voices, filling their own creative play with dialogue. That is why I have placed dialogue and voice first in this section. My concerns here are to encourage the playful use of language, and to harness that playfulness in developing literacy.

17

The material on dialogue and voice suggested in this chapter is all based on task-driven exercises, which encourage children first and foremost to play with language, to listen to the sounds and rhythms of words. The exercises can easily be adapted and integrated into process drama, examples of which can be found in *The Kraken, The Arrival* and *The Fall of Troy* projects.

Dialogue and theatre

In theatre, dialogue is spoken to be heard by an audience. In process drama the participants alternate between being actors and audience, sometimes doing both at the same time; they are their own audience. That does not, however, make the need for precision in language any less important.

Well written dialogue carries multiple meanings. What are the functions of dialogue in a play?

- what a person says and the way that they says it tells us about their attitudes, their state of mind, their thoughts, their emotions, their hopes and fears, desires and dreads, their personality

- it can give similar information about other characters

- it can imply or provide information about situations – what has happened elsewhere or at an earlier time can suggest what might happen in the future

- in scripted plays, dialogue can also imply stage action. 'Don't come any closer' implies that the other person is threatening to do just that

- dialogue is also the means by which ideas are explored, through which opposing views can be set against each other and meanings teased out.

It would be wholly inappropriate to tell a class that you expect them to write dialogue which does all that when they start to create their own short plays. But you should bear this rich potential in mind when you respond to their work – whether it's as part of a process drama or when hearing or reading short plays they have written. We will return to this later in this chapter.

Practical Work

These tasks and exercises are designed to encourage children to play with dialogue, to explore different voices. You might want to use them on their own, or as part of a more extended scheme of work in literacy and/or drama. They can be worked on as a whole class, by small groups or by individuals, once they have had plenty of experience.

Most of them can be adapted for use in a process drama by placing the activity within the context of a developing dramatic fiction – see below.

- photocopy a picture book, blanking out the written text. Add dialogue boxes in comic-book style. Children fill in the dialogue. This allows you to ask questions about the way people speak, the kind of vocabulary they use

- complete missing dialogue from a story book

- Take a known story and ask what the characters might say, and how they might say it in situations other than those presented in the original. See *Not Now Bernard, The Pet Cellar, Wolves in the Walls, Voices in the Park*

- the whole group collaborates with the teacher in constructing a character, which the teacher could then take on in a developing drama. 'How do you want me do this? What should s/he say now? How should s/he say it? Let's try it out.' This could be developed through Forum Theatre, the resulting dialogue written down. See *Not Now Bernard, The Pet Cellar, The Arrival, The Fall of Troy.*

Camouflaging dialogue

Camouflaging: the concealing of things by disguising them to look like their surroundings.

The following exercise is useful in developing many literacy skills, not only those immediately relevant to play writing. Although the task seems simple, it can lead to remarkably sophisticated writing.

The children are arranged in pairs. Each pair is given two lines of dialogue, for example:

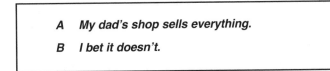

> A   *My dad's shop sells everything.*
>
> B   *I bet it doesn't.*

The exercise is to write another six lines of dialogue around these two lines. The given dialogue can be placed anywhere, but it has to be retained word for word and in the order as given. The resulting eight line play is then read aloud or performed with the intention of camouflaging the original dialogue so that the given lines will not be recognised.

Here is one way in which these two lines might be developed:

> **A** My dad runs the shop
>
> **B** So? My dad's a builder
>
> **A** My dad builds his own shelves
>
> **B** My dad built the channel tunnel
>
> **A** *My dad's shop sells everything*
>
> **B** *I bet it doesn't*
>
> **A** Does
>
> **B** Bet it doesn't sell packed lunches

The exercise encourages participants to

- pay close attention to the voice of each character (rhythm, vocabulary, register)
- speculate about who these people might be and about the situation in which this dialogue occurs
- improvise or write in the voice of the written character
- pay close attention to each others' work in performance because the audience also has a task: to identify the given lines in the eight line plays.

In the form presented above, the exercise is probably more appropriate for older children, but in my experience it engages most children, including those who have problems putting pencil to paper in more traditional writing exercises, providing it is tackled in an appropriately supportive way. With any class, when first presenting the work, it would probably be best to introduce the exercise to the whole group, and discuss how it works, with the teacher writing down suggestions.

Useful questions might include:

- who do you think is involved in the scene? How old do you think they are?
- what are they/have they been talking about?
- have they been talking before they say the given lines?
- what do you think might have happened before the scene starts?
- Where do you think it's happening?

Some children will find it easier to improvise, using the given lines as a starting point; others will enjoy discussing the problem and teasing it out on paper. The exercise also lends itself to children working collaboratively with the teacher, with the teacher taking on one of the roles and asking what kind of things you should say, enabling you to draw specific attention to elements of, for example:

- vocabulary – What kind of words would she use? Long words, posh words, slang?

- speech rhythms – Short clipped sentences, or longer, more discursive? Leaving out verbs?

- tone – Non committal? Enthusiastic? Emotional?

- register – Formal, informal?

Photocopiable dialogue extracts for use in the camouflaging dialogue exercise can be found in Section Four, Resources.

Responding to the work

The task as presented has an element of competition about it – can each group conceal the given dialogue from others in the class? It is therefore important to prevent those pair groups who do not immediately succeed in the task from feeling disheartened by their apparent failure – not least because that sometimes creates more opportunities for learning than the successes. If the given dialogue is relatively easy to identify within the camouflaging text, that allows you to open up discussion about, for example, the appropriateness of particular vocabulary, or the different ways that people use language in different social situations. Groups which don't succeed in the primary task of camouflaging their given dialogue, should be praised for other elements of their work. The great joy of the exercise is that it encourages children to play with language. It also encourages discussion about meaning with even those children most lacking in literacy confidence. Children are often good at identifying the given lines but find it much more difficult to say anything more than that 'they just seem different from the others'. Responding to the work allows you to introduce issues of voice: choice of vocabulary, speech rhythms, tone and register.

Bearing in mind the various functions of dialogue in theatre, discussions of the work should also refer to the characters and the content of the scene. In effect this becomes a kind of light touch textual analysis.

Adapting and developing the exercise

In the example given above, I have attributed the lines to A and B in order to allow children to name the characters. Younger children are likely to find this conceptually difficult, so you could attribute the lines to the icon of a character. Thus:

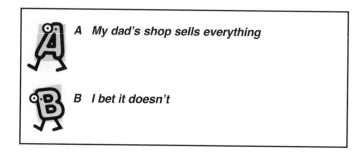

Or

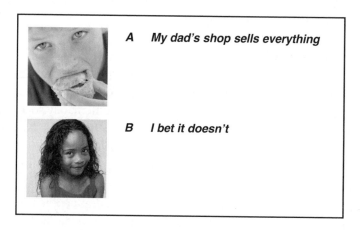

If you want to give the children more guidance, you might identify the characters by name, as they usually are in a play text.

The camouflaging dialogue exercise can be used in a wide variety of different contexts, and for various different purposes.

It can also be used to introduce stories and reading books, generating curiosity and encouraging children to be active, imaginative, speculative readers. An example of this is given in the *Wolves in the Walls* project, where children are given dialogue extracts from the book before they've read it, and encouraged to play with the dialogue, making up their own scenes from a two line starting point, discussing a possible sequence of scenes, and then speculating about the content of the book from which it comes.

Matching dialogue

The dialogue exercise can also be adapted and used as a kind of game. The class is divided into two groups, A and B. Each person in each group is given a single line of dialogue. They then have to find someone else from the other group who has a line with which theirs will work as a pair. If you have an odd number of children in the class, you can join in yourself.

When everybody has a partner, hear the results. Talk about which pairings work and which seem to make less sense. As with camouflaging dialogue, those which are superficially the least successful often provoke the most interesting discussions. Indeed, another way of using the exercise is to ask the children to find a partner without even looking at their own line, and then to try to make sense of the resulting exchange.

Example:

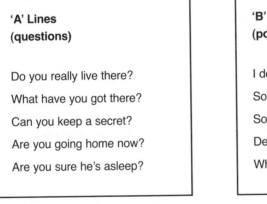

'A' Lines (questions)	'B' Lines (possible responses)
Do you really live there?	I don't know.
What have you got there?	So what if I do?
Can you keep a secret?	Sometimes.
Are you going home now?	Depends.
Are you sure he's asleep?	Who've you been taking to?

As with all these tasks and exercises, there are no right or wrong responses. Even the most unlikely sounding match can provoke fascinating discussion.

Extracts for this exercise, graded for difficulty, can be found under the heading *One Line Matches* in the photocopiable resources in Section Four.

Having found a pair to their own line of dialogue, they might add further lines of their own, thus developing the resulting pair into a 6 or 8 line play.

Missing Lines

An exercise for Upper Primary.

The children are given three lines of unattributed dialogue.

They have to look carefully at the lines for clues: Who might be speaking? Where are they? What's been happening?

Then write a short exchange of dialogue in which these lines appear. They have to come in the order as given, but they can appear anywhere in the dialogue, as stand alone lines, or as part of longer lines.

It's very important in setting up this exercise that you don't give the impression that there's a right answer. It's a problem, and there are numerous ways of tackling it.

Given lines

    the dog was lying on your bed

    football practice

    it will be

Resulting dialogue

Mum	When I got home this afternoon **the dog was lying on your bed**
Tom	That's not my fault
Mum	You know she makes the bedclothes filthy
Tom	I'm sorry, Mum. I had **football practice**. I forgot to shut my door. Is tea ready?
Mum	**It will be** when you've taken her for a walk

Extracts for the Missing Lines exercise are provided in the photocopiable resources in Section Four, p184.

Developing playscripts

All these tasks and exercises value economical writing. The concept of the eight line play is as liberating as it is constraining. It's not only children who ramble when asked to improvise in drama. The focus here is on precision in language, whilst actively promoting playfulness. The material in Section Three includes many examples when you might ask children to write short dialogues for different purposes such as summarising events or as a starting point for other kinds of work.

It is, however, also possible to develop these short plays further. The key is to seek development through structured tasks. One way is to see the six-to-ten line play as a scene from a larger play. In the first instance it's best to limit the number of characters to those who appear in the original. The chapter on *Structure, narrative and story telling* offers suggestions about shaping this development. But essentially, you are asking

- **who** are the people in this scene?
- **where** are they?
- **what** has happened before this exchange?
- what's **at stake** for them here?
- **how** might they resolve it?

Process drama

As argued above, process drama provides an overarching fiction which should both engage children and provide them with protection. The participants may be part of the action, but they are also observers and interpreters of it; they step regularly in and out of role. In order to adapt any of the tasks and exercises in this chapter for use in a process drama, a fictional context is needed.

Examples

Indications of some of the ways in which an eight line scene might be integrated into a wider fiction.

Jack and the Beanstalk
Police investigation. Who overheard what the bean-seller said to Jack?

Not Now Bernard
Video recording of interaction between Bernard and one of his parents shown to experts trying to help Bernard's parents.

The Pet Cellar

Robert's message to the police or RSPCA, including his account of what Mr Creech said to him.

The Kraken

Transcripts of the spy's encounters with the carpenter.

Wolves in the Walls

Lucy re-enacting an exchange with a wolf for the benefit of her family or friends.

The Dunce

The enacted poem as video evidence in an investigation.

The Arrival

Summarising in no more than eight lines of dialogue any of the key events, social interactions and personal exchanges for use as exhibits in a Museum of Immigration.

The Fall of Troy

Memories of the dead soldier collected to honour him and create a memorial to him.

The Arrival and *The Fall of Troy* also contain examples of **collective speech writing**, where the class collaborate in order to write a persuasive speech, using methods which are effectively a development of the exercises suggested in this chapter.

Character and role

'The art of choosing just those details about a person which catch his or her life, is not an easy one ... The whole art of writing is to make your reader's imagination go into action.' (Ted Hughes, 1967:44)

Much has been written about the distinction between character and role in educational drama. The debates are usually couched along the following lines. The terms character and characterisation are usually associated with theatre, with performance. Characters may be complex, many sided and sometimes contradictory, but they have a solidity about them which is performable. A role is something that we take on, that we play, that we play with. In every day of our lives we play different roles at different times: in the afternoon we might be a teacher dealing with a worried parent, then go home and be a parent before visiting our own father, maybe assuming the role of the child.

It is, however, important to remember that characterisation in the theatre takes many forms. The 'well made play' was primarily driven by plot, its characters little more than devices. The characters may be readily identifiable but they are as fixed as they might be in a modern video game. Naturalist drama prides itself on characters that are more real to us because they are more psychologically complex. Much of the writing about characterisation in educational drama seems to allude to these two extremes. In many forms of theatre however, (from classical Greek, through the riches of the early seventeenth century to the present day) the personal psychology of a character is far less important than the interaction between that character and their social and political environment. It is those social interactions which concern us in educational drama and which drive process drama.

In process drama, learning takes place when participants engage with the dramatic fiction in a way which demands that they are simultaneously responding *as themselves* and *in role*. They know that they have a responsibility for the developing fiction. If, as sometimes happens when children have no previous experience of the form, they hide behind the mask of a character, they lose that vital sense of themselves as makers in a collaborative process. The roles that participants adopt offer both pleasure and protection, enabling them to adopt the attitudes, opinions, points of view and responsibilities of others. They can then explore the implications and consequences of these without fear.

Not only is there no need for the child or the teacher to develop a character in the drama, to do so would be usually be inappropriate, shifting the focus from the collective to the individual. If, as teacher, you take on a role in the drama, you do so primarily to focus the work. Where you ask the class to construct you as a character, as described in the latter part of this chapter and in several of the projects, this is a collaborative process. You are working with the group, which effectively writes the character you will take on and then directs you in the role. The construction of the character is purposeful; and the *process* of collaborative construction is as important as the subsequent playing. The class, as *playwrights*, have made the character for you because that character has specific dramatic functions – usually an obstacle of some kind, so that they have to persuade you or negotiate with you. And you, the teacher, have adopted this technique in order to create specific learning opportunities.

When we watch a character in a play we expect a certain amount of consistency in their behaviour; if they behave in contradictory fashion we expect that to reveal an aspect, perhaps a flaw, of character or for it to expose some of the socio-political pressures bearing down on them. The roles that participants assume in a process drama are necessarily more fluid. We do not require the consistency we seek in theatrical characters. Indeed, we should actively encourage exploration of a range of attitudes, opinions and beliefs.

The role play in process drama is likely to range from taking on the general responsibilities and attitudes of, for example, museum curators in *The Arrival* to something more specific, such as the role of a miller in *The Kraken*. Even in this instance, however, you are not asking the child to develop a character for the miller but, rather, to view the events of the fiction from that point of view and to use the role to try out opinions and attitudes.

Whilst I wholeheartedly agree with these arguments that it is not only inappropriate but distracting and potentially destructive to focus on characterisation in process drama, the distinction is not always as clear as it is claimed. Providing we remember that process drama is necessarily a collaborative process and that it demands wise, creative *play*, then considering character in the way that a playwright might think about it can complement the other kinds of work we undertake in a process drama.

The tasks and exercises below are primarily aimed at developing an awareness of and respect for the complexity of people and the ways that thought, feeling, actions and social environment interact. They will help children develop literacy skills. And, like all the work in this section, they can be adapted for use in process drama.

Practical Work

The following are adapted from exercises in Noel Greig's book *Playwriting* which he specifically devised for use in primary schools. 'The investigation of what goes on inside is an invaluable way of extending the literacy of emotion, feeling and thought.' (Greig, 2005:14)

- place your hand on a piece of paper and draw the outline of it
- think of all the things your hand has done today: ordinary things, strange things, things you enjoyed, things you don't feel good about
- around the outside of the outline of the hand write five sentences, each beginning with the words 'today my hand'

Example:

Today my hand ...

    – stroked the dog

    – drew a rude picture of the teacher

    – did some Maths in the wet lunch break

    – played on my Play Station

    – tripped my friend in the playground...

The exercises can be used to open up a discussion of the way that people behave differently at different times, playing different roles depending on who we are with and where we are, that we can be loving, rude, conscientious, determined and mean all in the same day.

Role on the wall

This exercise can be used in conjunction with the hand, in its own right, as a way of focusing on characters in stories, or as a means of slowing down or developing a process drama.

- draw the outline of a person on a large sheet of paper

- on the outside of the outline write down some agreed facts and description about the character – for example with *Little Red Riding Hood*, you might write 'red boots', 'red cape', '10 years old', 'smiley face', 'she lives near a wood'
- on the inside, write what thoughts and feelings the person has – for example, 'she likes flowers', 'she feels lost', 'she is frightened of wolves'

Thus we are beginning to think about the difference between the way people appear and what they think and feel. When used as part of a process drama it provides a useful visual aid, a reference point to which you can return, adding or amending information as the drama develops.

The exercise is adapted near the beginning of the first part of *The Fall of Troy* project where the class focus on an outline drawing to represent a dead Greek soldier. In this context it also exemplifies the importance of activating the imagination of the participants. Had I dressed another teacher as the dead soldier in an elaborate costume resembling those depicted on Greek vases, or even hired a professional actor to play the role, it is likely that the interrogation of the image would have focused on its realism. With an outline drawn onto a piece of paper, there can be no question as to how realistic or not it is; the image and its context become active and resonant through the imagination of participants.

Having thought about possible relationships between outward appearances and thoughts and feelings, the internal and external world of a person, try going back to the hand exercise.

- on your piece of paper you should have five things that your hand did. Now add a feeling to each of these actions. Thus you have an action and a feeling.
- now add a thought that relates closely to the action

Getting at the difference between thoughts and feelings can be difficult, but essentially you are looking to end up with *what* was done (the action), *why* it was done (the thought) and the *result* (the feeling).

Example:

Thought	Action	Feeling
The dog looked miserable	I stroked the dog	I felt happy
I thought the teacher was getting at me	I drew a rude picture of the teacher	I felt naughty
I wanted to catch up with work	I did some Maths in the wet lunch break	I felt proud
I wanted to beat my own record	I played on my Play Station	I felt pumped up
I thought my friend was cheating	I tripped him in the playground	I felt guilty

For each of the actions, you now have the basis of a short story: 'I thought the dog was looking miserable, so I stroked her and felt happy'.

■ now try to do the same for a character in a story, such as Lucy in *Wolves in the Walls*

These exercise can also be used in conjunction with some of those in the chapter entitled *Observation*, particularly the *table of questions to develop character observation*, which also focuses on actions, thoughts, feelings, and on differences between private fears and shared fears.

■ now try to use dialogue to try to tell one of these stories. For some of them you will need to add another character, so instead of simply 'wanting to beat your own record' on the Play Station, you might have to persuade your Mum to delay the evening meal.

Using Forum Theatre to construct a character

This technique, which is used in several of the projects, involves the teacher offering to take on a role, but asking the class *how* she should do it. The more children you can involve in the process the better. Although you will be playing the role, they still have some ownership of it.

You might initially ask them to sculpt you into a still image of the character; and then discuss body language, movement, language, vocabulary, register. Your questioning needs to be tuned to the abilities and needs of the class; and ideally the character should be constructed for a specific purpose.

Constructing a character in this way enables you, the teacher, to take on the role and use it in the drama in one-to-one exchanges, with small groups or as part of a larger process drama. Because the construction of the character has been a collaborative process in which the children have participated, they have a degree of control over the character which makes it possible to make the character more aggressive, more frightening, more challenging than if the teacher presented the role cold. A good example of this can be found in *The Pet Cellar* project.

Process Drama

In process drama, the Stanislavskian concept of characterisation, where character tends to be thought of in psychological terms, is rarely appropriate. But this is not always the way that the notion of character works in theatre. And there are strategies used by playwrights which can easily be adapted by drama teachers and used as powerful learning tools.

In terms of characterisation, all playwrights work with stereotypes. When we watch a play for the first time, we recognise characters as types, we quickly develop expectations, anticipating they will behave in certain ways. This is as true of plays by the greats as it is of plays we might dismiss as shallow and un-important. At first sight Hamlet is a troubled revenger, Madame Ranyevskaya in Chekhov's *The Cherry Orchard* an emotional widow, Brecht's Mother Courage a working mother.

To anyone who knows these plays, the descriptions will seem irritatingly simplistic. But whereas poor playwrights allow the stereotype to remain un-challenged, a good playwright works *with* audiences' expectations, not by pandering to them, but by acknowledging them and then challenging or even shattering them.

When we first encounter any theatrical character, our reading of them neces-sarily draws on our previous cultural experiences. When the ghost of Hamlet's father emerges from the mists on the battlements at Elsinore, the apparition may shock Horatio and the Officers of the Watch, but it is likely it would have delighted audiences at The Globe at the end of the sixteenth century, for it would have triggered expectations of a bloody revenge tragedy – which is what Shakespeare gives them, though not quite in the way they might have anticipated.

So although our immediate response may be superficial, it is nevertheless an important stage in the process by which meaning is created. And just as the playwright works with cultural familiarities in order to probe deeper, to challenge and to ask difficult questions, so too the teacher working on process drama has to work *with* the participants' cultural interests and expectations. If you adopt a role in process drama, it needs to be one which the class can readily identify and to which they can quickly respond. As the drama develops and the children become more engaged with the dramatic fiction, the function of the role is likely to change.

Early on in the drama, you might use the role to inform, establish context, model language registers or offer support to the participants. Later you might use it to control structure, pace, dramatic tension, rhythm; to introduce elements of surprise; and, as the children confidence grows, to provoke and challenge. And in parallel with these, the children's roles will also change. Many of these shifts can be seen in *The Kraken* and *The Arrival*. In both these projects the teacher takes on low status roles and, as the drama develops, the class are encouraged to interrogate their own responses and interactions.

At the beginning of the chapter *Dialogue and Voice*, I referred to the usual approach in playwriting courses being one where participants are encouraged to work on character and story before trying to write dialogue. If you wish to use some of the playwriting exercises suggested in this book in conjunction with process drama, it is best to allow the drama to provide you with the people and their situation rather than starting with any of the character exercises suggested in this chapter and trying to develop process drama out of them. If you do choose to use character work within a process drama, you need to situate it within the context of the dramatic fiction. In *The Arrival*, for example, much time is spent exploring the social context of the emigration, considering those episodes in the lives of the emigrants which forced them to leave the old country and speculating about the forlorn lonely figure on the deck of the ship clinging to his suitcase.

In a process drama, character work might take the form of personal diaries, letters, interviews, writing CVs, constructing characters. At a later stage, all of these activities could be drawn on to develop short plays or used as a basis for other kinds of literacy activities.

Teaching in role

Given the provisos discussed above about constructing a character for specific purposes, the teacher working in role should not be performing a character; the prime purpose is not to entertain but to engage the students more actively in the process. There may be an element of performance, but it is closer to the way in which we perform versions of ourselves in different social situations than to the performance of an actor in the theatre.

Much has been written about teaching in role. And I do not have anything further to add here, except to recommend specific books, where the strategy is described and analysed in far more detail than I have space for here. Full publication details for these books can be found in the *Bibliography*.

- *Teaching Drama* by Morgan and Saxton p38-66

  Specific chapter on teaching in role offers a detailed account of the functions and kinds of role with pragmatic but thoughtful analysis of associated advantages and disadvantages

- *Structure and Spontaneity: the process drama of Cecily O'Neill*, edited by Taylor and Warner

  References to teaching in role throughout the book, but the chapter entitled *Alienation and Empowerment* (p141-149) offers very useful insights into the power of irony in theatre and process drama

- *The Teaching of Drama in the Primary School* by Brian Woolland, p55-61.

  A brief summative account, categorising by status and function and offering practical advice to the beginner

The following books refer to teaching in role throughout, and are strongly recommended.

Acting in Classroom Drama: a Critical Analysis by Gavin Bolton
Dorothy Heathcote: Drama as a Learning Medium by Betty-Jane Wagner
Drama Worlds: A Framework for Process Drama by Cecily O'Neill

Structure, story and narrative

D rama and story are not the same thing, although drama is often used to tell stories and stories are often adapted into drama. How are they different? They do share many elements, most importantly characters and narrative. A dictionary definition of drama proposes that it is a 'story ... related by means of dialogue and action.' But in drama, stories are often implied, rather than related; and the definition is misleading in its suggestion that the prime function of drama is to tell stories. In order to dramatise a story we need to focus on particular moments. Whereas a story is likely to be filled with incident, drama teases out the meanings in social interactions and exchanges. It may not be a workable definition of drama, but it is certainly a characteristic of good educational drama that it dwells on the moment. In their own creative dramatic play, children tend to rush things. One of the teacher's jobs is to slow things down in order to explore the details of human interactions. Edward Bond has coined the term **Accident Time** in relation to his own theatre; and it is an extremely useful concept in educational drama.

> This composite word expresses the particular nature of time when an accident occurs ... Bond deliberately intermingles two very different events – a car accident and a cyclone – and merges them into a single metaphor. In the same way that a victim of an accident has the impression that time suddenly slows down, anyone who finds themselves in the eye of a cyclone is struck by the stillness there, contrasting greatly with the furious speed of the whirlwind all around. In both cases, the key thing for Bond is the contrast between the calm of the centre and the violence and chaos surrounding it. As a result there is a precision of perception, an enhanced 'clairvoyance', of the details of the events which are happening. Transposing this double phenomenon into theatrical representation, Bond places the audience in accident-time, inside a theatrical cyclone which is dramatic action, echoing the turbulence and accidents of life. The audience is therefore in the paradoxical situation of benefiting from the protective calm of the centre the better to analyse the nature and implications of the tumultuous or tragic events in which they find themselves plunged. (Davis, 2005:201)

Whether we are engaged in a large process drama project or working with a small group of children on their own play, it's important to investigate the ordinary, slowing things down in order to seek meaning in what appears commonplace.

Drama and change

It has often been argued that drama is underpinned by high conflict and confrontation. The colloquial use of the word drama as being something which is several rungs up from a crisis implies this vernacular sense that being dramatic is an over-reaction. Much drama is indeed concerned with confrontation, but the function of conflict in drama is always as a catalyst. It is not conflict that makes a situation dramatic, but the *potential for change* that the conflict triggers. Confrontation only creates the possibility for drama when it raises the possibility of change of some kind. This does not mean that the characters or the situation necessarily do change. Our interest is engaged by wanting to know whether they will. There are numerous very fine plays in which the characters resist or refuse change, but it is still the *possibility* of things being other than they are that makes the situation dramatic and engages us in the drama.

Every moment in a play or a drama is about change, or contains the potential for change. Those changes might be major or apparently trivial, but without the potential for change there is no drama. Consider a couple of children stuck in an argument:

- You tore my coat
- No I didn't
- Yes you did
- No I didn't ...

There is conflict and confrontation here, but it only becomes dramatic when the possibility of change arises, when one of them hesitates or backs down or tries to change the subject, when we glimpse the possibility of a resolution. The short scene about Dads in the chapter **Dialogue and Voice** is dramatic because the two children are each trying to impress each other, because each has to change in order to accommodate the other. Change can happen in many different ways, as indicated in the following tables. The examples are not exhaustive. You will find many more examples of change and potential change in the practical projects than are documented below, and the suggested categories of change frequently overlap.

Change	Examples
Affecting individuals	Teacher in role persuaded by group – *The Arrival, The Fall of Troy*
Affecting small groups	*The Kraken.* Groups discuss how to deal with the carpenter
Affecting communities and societies	*The Arrival.* Emigrants moving from the Old Country, travelling across the sea, then arriving and settling in a New World

Change can be internal or external. Internal changes may not always be apparent to others, whereas external changes are.

Internal changes include:

Change	Examples
Attitude	*Voices in the Park.* The young people overcome the prejudice of Mummy
Mood	*The Pet Cellar.* Robert overcomes his fear
Point of view	*Voices in the Park.* Events seen from different perspectives
Heart	*Jack and the Beanstalk.* Jack's Mum stops thinking of Jack as a waster
Mind	*The Fall of Troy.* Odysseus's speech persuading the Greeks not to desert
Belief	*The Kraken.* The villagers' beliefs about the Kraken change as they begin to understand about the threat of bacteria
Affection	*Not Now Bernard.* The class working to teach Bernard's parents how to give him more attention

External changes include:

Change	Examples
Circumstances – family, economic, friendship, health	*Jack and the Beanstalk*, *The Arrival*, *Wolves in the Walls*
Status	*Wolves in the Walls*. Family change from being householders to homeless.
Loyalty	*The Arrival*. Loyalties of immigrants tested when they get to the New World.
Fortune	*The Arrival*. Difference between expectations and reality on arriving in the New World.
Security	*The Fall of Troy*. Trojans under siege.
Role	*The Dunce*. How to enhance the Dunce's self-esteem so he no longer needs to play the class clown?

External changes will sometimes result in internal change, and vice versa.

The tables above refer to changes that take place, or could take place, within the fiction of the drama – to characters, to groups, to societies. But there are other crucially important changes that are integral to the processes of theatre and drama: the changes in an audience or, in the case of process drama, the participants. Brecht wrote of his intention to use theatre to make the familiar seem strange, to enable people to look at their social and political environment as if through the eyes of a stranger. It's a very productive way of thinking about educational drama.

With regard to educational drama it is essential to think about change when giving feedback to children as about their own plays. 'The playwright David Hare once said, 'never allow a character to leave a scene the same way as they entered it.' There is always some shift, even if it is a slight one' (Greig, 2005:89-90).

It is very useful to bear this in mind if you are working in process drama, where one of the responsibilities of the teacher is to create situations in which change and learning, itself a kind of change, are possible for the participants – both in themselves and in the roles they have taken on in the drama. At risk of being reductive, the attempt to solve a problem in role is what provides the focus in a process drama; and can itself be seen as an attempt to effect change.

Practical Work
Scripts and storyboards

A play text can be an attempt to record a drama or guidance as to how to perform it. A script which notes the spoken dialogue is only one way of doing this. Plays and dramas can be recorded and annotated in other ways. Film scripts are usually developed through storyboards, and in the theatre, where spoken language is only one of the theatrical languages at work, storyboarding is sometimes also used in development, particularly in more experimental and physical forms of theatre.

It is argued that reading and writing are central to the National Curriculum because without them it is impossible to learn in other areas. The evident truth of this does, however, ignore the extent to which our society has become a culture dominated by juxtapositions of written, visual and aural languages. If learning to read is important, then so too are the skills of making and decoding visual texts. There are times when it is more appropriate and more useful to make a visual representation of the scenes, or units of action, that comprise the drama than it would be to write them up in the form of dialogue.

Storyboarding and sequencing

As a classroom activity, storyboarding – telling a story in pictures, much as in a comic strip – can be a very useful activity, which can either precede or follow on from making sequences of still images in drama. Adding captions to each frame in the storyboard to summarise the story can offer a means of reflecting on a narrative. Adding dialogue in comic strip boxes can provide a strong visual means of recording a basic script. Editing an extended scene down to just one line of dialogue for each participant in the scene is an important skill in its own right.

The exercise of storyboarding is also useful at a more sophisticated level, when working with much older groups as a means of seeking out the structure of a scene, whether the group is realising an existent text or devising the scene.

In developing a sense of dramatic structure it is useful to think in terms of an odd number of scenes. Starting with 3 gives a clear sense of a beginning, a middle and an end. This can then be developed into 5 scenes or images (see page 40).

If the first frame is the beginning of the play and the third is the middle, the second connects the two; similarly the fourth, the middle and the end. In this

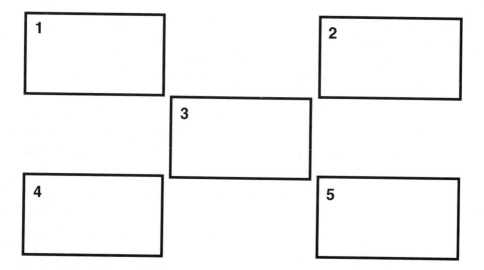

way a short scene of few lines can be developed not only into a longer scene, but also into a sequence of scenes. The key is always to break work down into manageable tasks. An example of developing a short scene into a longer play can be found in *The Dunce*.

Creating a storyboard focuses on a key aspect of narrative: the way that sequencing produces meaning. If you change the order in which events occur, you change the relationship between them, change our understanding of how and why things happened they way they did. The *Oxford Dictionary of Literary Terms* refers to plot as the 'pattern of events and situations in a narrative or dramatic work ... arranged ... to emphasise relationship – usually of cause and effect – between incidents....'

Exercise

Make photocopies of images from a picture story book or graphic novel and ask the children to place them in an order which tells a story. Alternatively, take dialogue extracts from the story and ask children to place these extracts in order. How does the story change if you change the order? See examples in: *Jack and the Beanstalk, Wolves in the Walls, The Arrival.*

Exercise

The following exercise, which is adapted from an exercise in Noel Greig's, *Playwriting* (Greig, 2005:32-4) is useful both for thinking about plot and structure and for generating material for short plays. It can be tackled by groups – or individuals if they are confident.

A journey to school
Part 1

1. Think of the journey you make between your own front door and the door of your classroom when you come to school..

2. Write down, in order, seven things that you saw, heard or did along the way. Think of the journey as a washing line, with the seven things pegged out along it. These things don't have to be major events, they can be very ordinary.

3. Create a seven frame storyboard with very simple drawings in each of the seven frames. The drawings can be like stick pictures. Add short captions to each picture. Lay the pictures out as if they were hanging on a time line.

Part 2

4. It is quite likely that your journey was quite ordinary. So look along the time line and find somewhere to substitute one of your pictures with one that *didn't* happen. This imagined thing should be unusual, mysterious, puzzling, thought-provoking or worrying; but be sure to keep it believable, something that *could* have happened.

5. Add another person, related to the new event, into the new picture. Make sure the new person is believable. Avoid fantasy: alien visitations, pop stars, famous footballers or film stars.

6. Rewrite the final part of the story from the new event. Allow it to go where it needs to, adding pictures as needs be; but you should still end it by arriving at the door to the classroom.

7. Write a short dialogue for two of the characters in one of the pictures...

Example – Part 1

Here is an example as told by a teacher:

1. **I leave my house** and lock my front door behind me.
2. I take the wheelie bin in from the street.
3. I call in to the newsagent to buy a paper.
4. **I'm reading the paper and not looking** where I'm going and nearly walk into a lamp-post.
5. I put the paper in my bag and pay more attention to where I'm going.
6. As I walk through the school gates, the caretaker nods at me but doesn't say hello.
7. **I arrive at the classroom.**

Examples – Part 2

Everything stays the same until I nearly walk into the lamp post:

- **I'm reading the paper and not looking where I'm going and ...**

    - I trip over a dog tied up to a lamp-post and cut my hand

    - I have an argument with the owner

    - we both apologise

    - I get to school, but there's nobody in the playground because I'm so late

    - **I arrive at the classroom**, where the Headteacher is looking after my class...

    - **I'm reading the paper and not looking where I'm going ...**

    - when someone taps me on the shoulder

    - I turn round and it's the shopkeeper who gives me the change I've left on the counter in the shop

    - I'm really grateful to him

    - when I get to school, I'm so pleased about what happened that I go over and tell the caretaker what happened

    - the caretaker and I have a lively conversation – the first time I've talked to him properly

    - **I arrive at the classroom**, and I'm in such a good mood that I ...

Maps as storyboards

The exercise of making a storyboard from an everyday journey is a way of visualising a personal chronology. The storyboard thus becomes a kind of map of a personal journey which marks not geographical or spatial relationships, but those between emotional high spots. It also provides a way of writing about drama which draws attention to point of view. This concept of personal and emotional maps is very useful in drama. They can:

- focus reflection – as in *The Arrival*, where the class might use it to chart their journey from the old world to the new

- deepen understanding of the people involved in a drama – *Wolves in the Walls*, where the class think about Lucy's world away from the family house

- widen the frame of the drama – *The Pet Cellar*, where groups reconstruct Robert's journey from school to pet shop

- develop commitment to a situation – *The Fall of Troy*, where groups create an emotional map of the life of an unnamed soldier
- slow down the drama – *The Fall of Troy*, where the exercise is used to enable the dramatisation of a moment of violence

Structure and rhythm

Sequencing may be the prime consideration when thinking about dramatic structure, but it is not the only one. Rhythm is also very important. By rhythm I mean changes of:

- tone – for example, alternating a humorous scene with something more serious or sombre

- dialogue – short clipped sentences, or longer, more complex

- length of scenes – alternating short and long

- pace – the speed at which scenes are played

- dramatic tension – moments of high tension, moments of relative calm

The need to control rhythm is as important in children's plays and process drama as it is in the professional theatre. It is not simply about engaging and holding an audience's or the participants', attention, but also about meaning itself.

Although it sounds as if it is a sophisticated and challenging concept for primary age children, they are capable of playing with rhythm and manipulating it, providing the tasks are appropriate. In the dialogue extracts given for the camouflaging dialogue exercise, you will find several pairs in which one character says a lot, the other very little. If the camouflaging exercise is well handled, the speech rhythms in the extract will be replicated in dialogue written by the children.

Example:

A   Sugar's not fattening. I know it's not fattening. I know.

B   Who says?

When children are developing their own plays, you might suggest that they try to make each character sound different, for example:

- through different speech mannerisms – considering the different expressions that people use

- through different levels of articulacy – when one character speaks they might only use a few short words, or clipped sentences, while the other character speaks in complete sentences

- through different levels of vocal energy – one character a chatterbox, the other more shy

- in the way they use language – one perhaps speaking in formal English, the other in slang or dialect.

- if you are working with a class in which there are children for whom English is not their first language, they might write plays in which one character uses their first language.

In each of these cases, you are asking the children to play with language, and through their play to represent the spoken word.

If the children are making their own plays, using the five frame storyboard model, add constraints or suggestions such as:

- at least one of the five scenes to have no more than six lines of dialogue, and at least one of them to have ten or more

- at least one of the five scenes to be very tense, at least one to be more light hearted

- at least one of the scenes to include a long silence while we wait for one of the characters to make a decision

Working with stories

For teachers who have had little experience of drama, working with stories with which they and the children are familiar offers a secure starting point. The problem with enacting known stories is that we and the children already know how they end, and thus we lose dramatic tension. But there are other ways of manipulating dramatic tension. When we go see plays in the theatre or on television we sometimes know what's going to happen; when the structure relies on flashback, for example, or when we see a familiar play in a new production, but our interest is retained by the exploration of human behaviour in social contexts, by the how and why of people doing what they do.

Using known stories

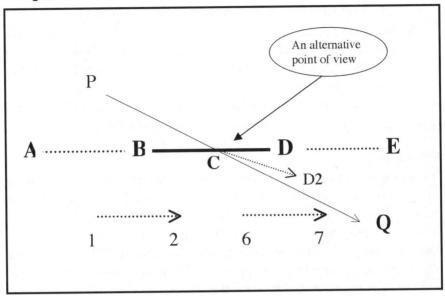

- enact the story, from **Beginning to enD** in the diagram. Techniques for enlivening this enactment are demonstrated in the projects *Jack and the Beanstalk* and *The Dunce*.

- locate our drama in what Hollywood calls the 'back story', A to B. In *Jack and the Beanstalk*, for example, what work have Jack and his mother tried to get themselves out of poverty before they have to sell their cow?

- if the children are not familiar with the story, as in *The Pet Cellar* and *Wolves in the Walls*, we can read them the story, but stop before the written end (at **C** on the diagram for example) and work with the **children** to **create their own ending** (**C** to **D2**).

- we can explore the lives of **characters whose stories run parallel** with those in our original story, looking at what's going on elsewhere while the well known story's taking place (**1** to **2**, **6** to **7** in the diagram). In *The Fall of Troy*, for example, a whole strand of work focuses on the Greeks waiting on the shore outside Troy while Achilles, Agamemnon and Odysseus decide what to do. In this respect it follows the lead of Aeschylus who dramatised the war 'not from the point of view of an aristocratic hero as in Homer, but from the standpoint of a disillusioned common soldier' (Wiles, 2000:98).

- we can move people **from offstage** in the known story to the centre of our drama, exploring how their stories intersect with the known story

(**P** to **Q**). Taking this approach might lead us to explore the wood-cutter's perspective on the events of *Little Red Riding Hood*.

- ■ we can look back at the events of the given story from **an alternative point of view**, giving us a different **dramatic frame**. Thus, if we were working on the *Pied Piper of Hamelin* our drama might be framed as **investigation** into how the corrupt town council came to hire the piper, with children creating documentary evidence before an enquiry. The concept of the dramatic frame is discussed on p122-123.

Sharing work

These thoughts and exercises about structure, story and narrative have been focused primarily on children's work as playwrights. But that all begs the question: if they write plays, however short, how are those plays to be shared with others? Reading and interpreting each others' plays creates wonderful opportunities for learning about drama, about language and literacy. In some of the tasks and exercises proposed in other chapters, sharing work is built into the exercise; the audience has a clear task when watching camouflaged dialogue, for example. There are, however, serious logistical and organisational problems in setting up small group work for the whole class and then looking at each group's work in turn. This can be very time consuming and often results in unproductive competition between groups and individuals. One way of dealing with the problem is for you, the teacher, to work closely with one group at a time while the rest of the class are engaged in something needing minimal supervision. But there will still be times when you and the children will want to share work. It is therefore very important to encourage the audience to be sensitive and active participants in this process, rather than passive or judgemental commentators.

Process Drama

Sharing work in process drama

The other way of thinking about sharing work is to set up group playwriting in situations which offer the protection of a broader fictional context. If the groups *within the dramatic world* are asked to create performances which are given status and significance within and by the larger drama, they can then be read and interpreted within that same context. The performances might, for example, be reconstructions of overheard conversations, exhibits, videos or, as in *The Arrival* and the last part of *The Fall of Troy*, museum performances.

Because the children are engaged in the drama, when you all look at the work of one small group, you all have an interest in it. Furthermore, the overall drama may well change as a result of the experience of watching and interpreting any group's performance, the most positive form of reading in role. Potentially, this creates rich and deep work; it enables you to tease out meaning, to draw attention to details of rhythm, tone, vocabulary and register through the structure of the drama itself. You might for example ask, 'I wonder why she is so quiet here?' in a way which values the decision to stay quiet, which seeks meaning in the quietness rather than judging it, which enables the participants to see the *effect* of their decisions.

The audience thus has an interest in other people's work, they want to know what's happening. This is what we should be working towards when work is being shared: creating a desire to see other people's work because it matters within the drama, because everybody's work affects everybody else's in some way.

Teacher as playwright

In many ways the teacher functions much as a playwright does when working with a theatre company on a devised play. The responsibilities of the teacher include:

- planning the drama with a view to engaging the children in dramatic fiction and creating appropriate learning opportunities
- identifying appropriate roles for the children and the teacher(s)
- setting up clear and purposeful tasks within the fiction
- structuring the drama
- reflecting on the drama.

Structuring the drama entails creating, ordering and focusing units of action: the situations, exchanges, interactions and episodes. The structural considerations discussed in relation to the playwriting work you ask children to do all apply when working on a process drama. The teacher also needs to keep an eye on the longer term structure, creating narrative tension at particular moments, especially when the project continues over a period of several weeks, as in *The Kraken*, *The Arrival* and *The Fall of Troy*. Stopping the drama at a cliff-hanger moment of high tension and suspense is a powerful way of holding the participants' interest.

Whilst manipulating narrative through cliff-hanger suspense is a useful tool for the teacher, you should try to avoid getting trapped in a straightforward linear chronology. In process drama, the teacher should always be looking to encourage wider perspectives, to stimulate broader and deeper understanding and insights. These will often emerge from considering the events of the drama from alternative points of view. Drama allows us to move through time, to slow things down, to dwell on the present, to dig into the past and to move to the future. The relationship between episodes may or may not follow a linear chronology – sometimes they might offer parallel perspectives – but there should always be a connection between them. Thus each episode should be engaging in itself, but should also expand or deepen the meanings of those with which it connects.

This shifting of perspective is exemplified in the extended projects *The Arrival* and *The Fall of Troy*. Although the overall chronology in both of these is linear and forward moving, events are seen from different points of view in different episodes of the drama and there are several occasions where participants in the drama shift back and forward in time.

Teacher as narrator

Reflecting on the drama demands collaboration with the participants to explore and tease out meaning and insights. A powerful way for the teacher to enable and encourage reflection within the drama is by occasionally taking on the role of a narrator. The teacher as narrator is one of those nebulous roles, half in, half out of the fiction of the drama; but nevertheless very much a part of it, reflecting on things that have happened, moving them forward and drawing attention to specific contributions. The simple strategy of pulling story(ies) out of the various exchanges, interactions, events, explorations, enactments is pleasurable for the participants because it values their work, building their understanding of the significance of what they have done in the developing fiction and giving coherence to what can sometimes seem rather tangled and fragmentary.

Examples of the technique used in practice can be found in following projects:

- *The Kraken*
- *The Arrival*
- *The Fall of Troy*

Resources

The British Film Institute publish some excellent resource materials with storyboards for use in Primary Schools, including *LOOK AGAIN! a teaching guide to using film and television with three-to eleven-year-olds.* Chapter Three, *Moving Images and Literacy* is particularly relevant. See below – in Section Four, Resources – for further details.

Meanings beyond the literal

'It is one of those curious facts that when two things are compared in a metaphor we see both of them ... more distinctly...' Ted Hughes (1967:45)

In some ways all drama and theatre creates meanings beyond the literal. In the theatre we are conscious of the actor performing at the same time as we read the character they are playing; we see the stage as we read what is represented upon it. We never read any theatrical event at only one level – whether it is a performance in the National Theatre or an improvised exchange in the play corner of an infant classroom.

> The politician who talks about 'the ship of state' is speaking metaphorically. A metaphor treats one thing (a ship) as if it were another (the state or what sustains it). (All) ... plays have metaphoric dimensions. The ship which founders in the first scene of Shakespeare's *The Tempest* (1610/11) could itself be understood as 'a ship of state' – the aristocrats are notably incompetent in understanding or managing it. The scene is acting as a metaphor. (Wallis and Shepherd, 1998:135)

The stage itself becomes a space imbued with meaning. There may have been productions of *The Tempest* in which designers attempted to create real looking ships, but most modern productions, and certainly any in the early seventeenth century, are more likely to use simple props – rope, tattered cloth, rolling barrels – to represent the ship.

Exactly the same processes are at work when children are engaged in drama activities. In *The Kraken* a school bench stands for a cross, in *The Arrival* a suitcase represents the life history of a lonely old man; a chair covered with yellow cloth becomes a golden throne in *The Fall of Troy*; and in *Not Now Bernard* school furniture is arranged to signify Bernard's home. The teacher may present an image, as with the suitcase in *The Arrival*, but meanings accrue to it through the process of the drama itself. The collaborative play-writing of process drama involves a great deal more than improvising dialogue.

49

When most pre-school children engage in dramatic play, they use toys to stand in for people, they configure an imaginative representation of their world using whatever they can find. Not only do most young children get great pleasure from their metaphorical representations of their world, it is an important way for them to explore their interaction with it. Young children understand and love the monster in *Not Now Bernard* because it is a witty way of dealing with monstrous behaviour. The great pleasure of Anthony Browne's apes is that they are thoroughly human – in their flaws and failings, their dreams, their fears. *Voices in the Park* deals with snobbery, social prejudice, shyness and the fear of otherness. The metaphorical framework provides a protective shield from the difficulties of confronting these issues in the real world, whilst simultaneously allowing us to explore them in depth.

Education and creativity

Some of the meanings in Shakespeare's plays for early seventeenth century audiences are likely to have been similar to those we find in them; but others change. This is as true of the grand themes as it is of the small details. You only have to read any scholarly edition of any of the plays to realise the extent to which a modern reader is likely to miss some of the puns and political allusions, and fail to understand some of the jokes, the vernacular language and expressions. Fortunately, there is an enormous amount that we do understand.

But as social and political conditions change, so too does our larger understanding of the plays and our broader response to them. For hundreds of years *King Lear* was not performed; deemed too bleak, too cruel for the stage. It is only in the years since the Second World War that it has become accepted as a great stage play, relentlessly interrogating authority, justice and brutality (Foakes, 1993). The point here is not that Shakespeare's plays have universal meanings that miraculously lie in wait for us then leap across four hundred years to greet us, nor that they can mean all things to all people, but that the plays are profoundly rich and meaningful to us through our interaction with them; and that their meanings cannot be constrained either by Shakespeare himself or by academic critics.

Metaphorical meanings are not fixed, they exist in the spaces between us; they are a product of our interactions with each other and with our culture and our environment. Understanding and learning to play with this fluidity must be central to any education which values creativity, which styles itself as humanising. People with autism tend to have great difficulty with metaphorical concepts; it is one of the factors that make socialisation so problematic for them.

One of the reasons why theatre is often seen as so threatening by repressive regimes and reactionary ideologies is that an audience in the theatre is actively engaged in the meaning making process. It is impossible to contain and restrict the reactions that a play can provoke because its meanings cannot be predetermined. Meaning does not pass from playwright to director to actor to audience member in a tightly wrapped package. The French language is revealing here. In France the audience *assiste* at the performance of a play. The meaning of any play – even the shortest of improvised exchanges – is made in the spaces between writers, performers and audience. Playwrights are makers, but so are audiences. We sometimes emerge from the theatre or cinema asking, 'What did you make of that?' That word 'make' is telling. If when watching groups perform publicly you focus on the *meanings* of what they have done, the sharing of work can become an important part of a genuinely collaborative process. As readers in the broadest sense, we all become active participants in the meaning making process. Exploring meaning, negotiating meaning is central to educational drama. That is one of the reasons why, elsewhere in this book, I have put so much stress on *reading in role*. If education is to be humanising rather than repressive, then we need to give children every opportunity to exercise their ability to make meaning beyond the literal.

A note about terms

I have used the term metaphor very loosely thus far in this chapter, as a way of referring to all meanings beyond the literal. Whilst you would probably not want to teach children in Primary School the difference between metaphor and metonym, it is helpful to be clear in your own mind about the difference between them – not least because metaphor, metonym and symbol are such important concepts in theatre.

Figurative language – any non-literal use of language, usually having some kind of metaphorical meaning. Most slang is figurative. Much humour in children's literature arises out of deliberate misunderstandings of figurative language.

Metonym – where a thing, or an image of that thing, is used to stand for something with which it is normally closely associated. Thus, we talk of sweat meaning hard work; we talk of paying with plastic meaning a credit card; and in Britain we talk of Number Ten to mean the office of the Prime Minister or the government. Metonyms are frequently used in theatre. In the example of the staging of *The Tempest* cited above, the rope and the barrels become a metonym for the ship.

Metaphor – where a thing, a word or an image stands for something similar, or where similarities are claimed as in Shakespeare's 'All the world's a stage'.

Symbol – the word 'symbolism' is often used colloquially to mean anything with a meaning beyond the literal. In this colloquial sense a word or an image is symbolic when it implies something else in addition to its obvious and immediate meaning. A more precise way of thinking about symbolism is that it transforms experience into an idea, and that idea into an image – in such a way that the image is not tied down to the original idea. The symbolic image remains **active**. Thus it is not possible to define the meaning of a symbol precisely. It will mean many things at the same time. It has an unconscious aspect that is wider than metaphor which can never be precisely defined or fully explained.

Practical Work
How to teach meaning beyond the literal?
Understanding of metaphor, metonym and symbol is not a specific measurable competency – which, to be charitable, is perhaps why none of these words get any mention in the Primary National Strategy for literacy. Does this mean that children cannot be taught to use metaphor, that meaning beyond the literal is beyond them? Far from it. They use figurative language all the time; they create their own metaphors. Developing understanding of and facility with meaning beyond the literal is, however, vital in developing a creative, humanising curriculum.

Examples
I am not suggesting stand-alone tasks in this chapter. There are, however, numerous instances in the practical projects in Section Three where the focus is on exploring meanings beyond the literal. In most of the projects, learning opportunities are created through the teacher's questions, promptings and reflections on the work. The examples below are discussed in greater depth in the relevant chapter. For the sake of brevity I have not attempted to use the language I would use with the specified age group.

Jack and the Beanstalk

Questions which explore the different values that different people place on things can open up issues of meaning: 'What does the cow mean to Jack and his Mum?' 'What do the beans mean to them?'

With year 1 children you are not likely to discuss metaphors and symbols, but that is what your questioning is getting at. The beans might thus be a symbol of hope, of new life, of Jack's gullibility.

The question 'How can we show where the giant's house is?' opens up issues of representation.

Not Now Bernard

Issues of representation and signification.

How to represent the house?

Bernard's parents' DIY is a sign of their lack of attention to Bernard. What else might signify this?

The Pet Cellar

Questions about meaning and representation.

What might Robert's entry into the shop signify – to him, to his brother, to Mr Creech?

What might the blue egg signify?

How to represent the shop? The journey to the shop?

The Kraken

The evolution of a complex symbol over a period of time in a process drama.

In the early stages of the project the cross functions as little more than a marker for a meeting place; by the end of the project it has been invested with many other meanings. As one of the children said, 'That (cross) was the way things used to be.'

Wolves in the Walls

Figurative use of language – 'It's all over?'

Emotional maps of Lucy's journeys.

The Dunce

Issues of value and meaning. Task based playwriting and improvisation.

The poem includes the line 'He says yes to what he loves.'

What does he love? Dramatise a sequence of moments when the chosen object is important – for example when *The Dunce* was given a book as a present.

What is the significance of the object in each of the scenes? What does the object mean to each of the people in the scenes?

The Arrival

Issues of value, meaning and signification. Objects accruing meaning through shifting perspectives and changing use.

What do the immigrants have to leave behind? What do they take with them? Working on the significance of each of these.

Objects which develop meanings beyond the literal during the course of the drama: photographs, drawings, the old man's suitcase.

The Fall of Troy

This project includes many examples similar to the above. Also includes highly metaphorical use of imagistic language in extracts from *War Music* and *The Iliad*. Collaborative play making to work with these extracts and develop extensions to them.

Exploring the meaning of the dead soldier's life. Pictures, memories, precious objects.

Significance of objects in Troy.

Significance and classification of objects in archaeological dig in final part of project.

Observation

'I am a playwright. I show
What I have seen...'
from *The Playwright's Song*, Bertolt Brecht (1935)

D rama is centrally concerned with what it means to be human, with how we negotiate our sense of self in relation to others, with how we make sense of the world around us and our relationship to it; it is about our interaction with the world. But drama is more than that; it does not merely examine social behaviour, it has the potential to humanise. As Edward Bond has argued, 'We act with humanity when our imagination recognises imagination in others' (Bond, 1999).

Imagination and observation

Some people claim they have no imagination, or that they don't think of themselves as being imaginative. But as Ted Hughes observed in his book *Poetry in the Making,*

> We all tell stories ... In fact you could not live if you were not continually making up little stories. When you cross a road you hesitate and you make sure everything is clear. You do this because a little story has run along in your head and shown you a car coming, screeching its brakes, swerving to miss you, bouncing off the far wall, probably turning over three times and bursting its doors and spilling out people and collie dogs. ... Quite a hectic little tale. (Hughes, 1967:87)

As all too many parents know, young children sometimes don't hesitate before crossing roads. The problem is not that they don't tell themselves stories, or that they are unimaginative, but that they have little experience of the dangers of traffic. Unable to imagine what they have not observed, they cannot relate their imagination to the realities of crossing the road. Imagination and close observation are very closely linked. And this is as true of fantasies as it is of gritty soap operas. One of the reasons that stories such as *Not Now Bernard, Voices in the Park, Wolves in the Walls* and *The Arrival* are so engaging is that their highly imaginative worlds are rooted in insightful observations of human behaviour and real situations; they tell us about ourselves.

The roles that children take on in drama, the characters that they construct, are usually based on a combination of their own personal experiences, their direct observations of human behaviour and what they understand of the world second hand through various media. These stories may be fictional or non-fictional – for example historical dramas, newspaper articles – or a mixture of the two, such as *The Arrival*, which fictionalises real events.

Self expression and otherness

Developing active, compassionate imaginations must be central to any education. It is sometimes claimed that drama encourages self expression. There are certainly frequent occasions when drama not only enables children with poor self-esteem to express themselves and to have their contributions honoured. Those opportunities are immensely valuable both for them and for their peers. But we should never forget that drama is about social exchange and interaction, that *self expression* is only a part of a process that is essentially dialogic. There are dangers in placing too much emphasis on self expression if doing so is at the expense of collaborative interaction. This is especially so at a time when few children grow up in cohesive communities; when new technologies can make for increasing social isolation; when personal identity is seen to be a product of one's consumer choices.

I suspect that human beings have always feared otherness. The theme has always obsessed dramatists: vendettas, tribal wars, cycles of revenge arising out of that fear have been the subject matter of drama for at least as long as dramas have been recorded. But most of those dramas are addressing deep seated anxieties, not simply documenting it. Fearing otherness does not have to result in violence or prejudice, does not have to lead to the denunciation of difference. If we label all those who are not with us or like us as our enemies, then we condemn ourselves to alienated isolation and we detract from our own humanity.

Drama is potentially a dynamic social learning process; it offers opportunities through which we can tentatively reach out to understand others. Drama can directly address the fear of otherness. Trying to understand others, how people behave and why they behave the way they do, is as central to the craft of the playwright as an interest in colour and shape and light is to the painter.

Practical Work

In this context, observation can be seen as an important social skill. Social skills can certainly be learned; but I wonder whether they can be taught. As teachers, we can provide opportunities through which they might be developed. A dynamic process drama, in which children are deeply engaged, provides numerous such opportunities. Every time the teacher slows the drama down and reflects on meanings, she is drawing attention to the details of human behaviour, teasing out relationships between actions and consequences. Some children may refuse the learning opportunity; but if they have engaged in the fiction they have already taken a step in another's shoes, have begun to perceive situations from other points of view than the one with which they are familiar. Dramas on much smaller scales can also create opportunities for developing social and observational skills. Young children's imaginative play is almost always based on observation. If they play at shops, they are copying observed behaviour, usually taking on a more dominant role than the one they play when they visit a shop with a parent in the real world.

Many of the learning opportunities for developing observation skills will be created by the teacher's questions and responses to children's work. The following examples are discussed in depth in the relevant chapter.

Not Now Bernard

'If I'm going to be Bernard's Dad, *how* should I be hammering nails before Bernard comes into the room? How good am I at DIY? I wonder why I get so impatient with Bernard?'

Dramatising the story from other points of view.

Voices in the Park

Looking at each of the families at home:

How do the adults organise the space?

What are mealtimes like in each home?

How are meals served?

Where is the dog while the humans are eating?

The everyday story dramatised from different points of view.

The Kraken

Numerous questions asked by the teacher, but specifically those which ask the children about their observations of the teacher in role as the carpenter:

'Who do you think he is?'

'What have you noticed about him?'

Wolves in the Walls

Retelling or dramatising the story from other points of view.

The observation questionnaire adapted to develop an invented character based on a book.

The Dunce

The detailed enactment of the poem – all those questions asking about the details of behaviour.

The teacher asking the class to think about people who might have contradictory things to say about *The Dunce*, and then wondering why different people might see him in such different ways?

Character Observation Exercise

The following exercise is intended to encourage close observation and thinking about others, to kindle imaginative thinking about the children's own social world. It is a starting point, not a stand alone exercise. You should adapt and develop it in ways that are most appropriate for your class. You might want to use it to facilitate dramatic writing, to assist in developing small group improvisation work, or adapt the questions for use in a large group process drama to deepen in-role work.

The questionnaire formalises this link between observation and the imagination. With older children, after first working through the exercise on a whiteboard, you could ask them to tackle it individually; with younger children I would suggest you use it as a guide to thinking about characters – as in the *Voices in the Park* project.

The purpose of the questionnaire is to encourage thinking about strangers not just as others but as people, to develop powers of observation, and to stimulate the imagination within constraints. The information on the questionnaire moves from the real into the imagined, from observations of environment and behaviour to imaginative speculation about a real person and their social world. The first part of the questionnaire is concerned with observed behaviour, the second encourages inference, deduction and the imagination. The questions move from the general to the specific. The first group of questions, for example, makes reference to a 'sound that you associate with this person'. There is nothing particularly important about this per se – it's there to stimulate observational skills and try to make the image of the person more concrete. You might add other questions.

In the second part of the questionnaire, there are two key questions:

- What fear or anxiety might this person be willing to admit to other people?
- What fear or anxiety might s/he not be willing to admit to other people?

Drama of all kinds, whether in large theatres, tiny studios, on television or in classrooms is often, if not always, concerned with fear: conquering fears, dealing with anxieties, speculating about 'what if?' That is certainly true of the practical projects in this book, whether it's the light-hearted fantasy of *Wolves in the Walls*, the social anxieties in *Voices in the Park* or the darker fears of personal humiliation in *The Dunce*.

This pair of questions about fears and anxieties is particularly useful for drama. Taken together they get at the difference between what someone is prepared to share with others and what they might privately admit to themselves. This difference is not only central to most drama but is also an extremely important part of social education through the arts. Drawing attention to it in the safe, protected context of a drama is non-threatening and allows each child the space to see that they are not alone in harbouring fears and anxieties which if kept private can be so debilitating.

The questionnaire is not intended to be in any way definitive, but is presented as a suggestion of a kind of work which could be a useful way of developing skills related to playwriting or of deepening a process drama.

On the questionnaire reproduced below, I have filled in the responses boxes as an example. On the sheet which is reproduced in Section Four Resources below, the responses column has been left blank – and there is an extra box for **ADDITIONAL INFORMATION** and/or **QUESTIONS**.

A table of questions to develop character observation
Example

Thinking of a real person you have often seen, but never actually spoken to, answer the following:	
OBSERVED BEHAVIOUR	
Three short statements of fact	*She works in the corner shop at weekends*
	She is easy with young children, but shy with adults
	Her clothes are always colourful
A possession or item of clothing that you associate with this person	*A stud in the nose*
A sound that you associate with this person – but not something s/he says	*The till in the shop opening*
Something you *have* heard this person say	*'I can't tonight. I've got some coursework to finish.'*
A time of day	*Mid morning*
Who was s/he talking to? Or who do you think s/he was talking to?	*A friend, I think*
An object or item of furniture that you might associate with this person	*An old-fashioned bicycle*
WHAT YOU IMAGINE ABOUT THIS PERSON, BASED ON WHAT YOU HAVE OBSERVED	
Something that you *imagine* this person really wants to do in his/ her life; something that drives them. Could be rephrased as 'What do you imagine might make this person really happy?	*To get a place at art school*
A fear that this person might be willing to admit to other people	*That she will fail her A Levels*
A fear that s/he is *not* willing to admit to other people	*That she is not sufficiently talented to make it as an artist*

Something you might *imagine* someone saying to this person ...	'You can do better than working in a corner shop'
Who says this?	Her Dad
And what does the person reply?	'I don't want to get a 'proper' job'
And *where* does this happen?	In the kitchen

An adapted version of the questionnaire also appears at the end of the *Wolves in the Walls* project.

Suggestions for using and developing these exercise.

In this form, completing the questionnaire should result in two lines of dialogue. These could be developed into eight or ten line scenes, which could themselves become part of a short play.

Try to give a sense through the dialogue in these scenes of what has happened before, and an indication of who these people are. In order to do this effectively, it is worth asking:

- who are these people?
- what has happened before this exchange/conversation?
- what is significant for them in this exchange?
- what's at stake for each of them?

Used with a book, as in the *Wolves in the Walls* project, the questions may appear to function more like a comprehension test than observation as such, but they do encourage detailed thinking about character, and can provide a stimulus to opening up different points of view or developing roles and characters.

All the projects in Section Three potentially stimulate the development of observation skills. The following projects highlight this specifically.

- *Not Now Bernard*
- *Voices in the Park*
- *Wolves in the Walls*
- *The Dunce*

SECTION THREE

Practical projects

Choice of material

All the projects, except for *The Kraken*, are derived from published stories. This was a deliberate decision to ensure that the source content would be familiar to most readers, making the process of adaptation from story to drama as visible as possible. *The Kraken* also differs from the other projects in that it is an account of an extended process drama that took place over seven weeks with a Year 4 class. The other projects all draw on work with children, but do not attempt to give a documentary account of specific lessons taught. They offer various different approaches. Some, such as *The Arrival* and *The Fall of Troy*, are extended; some are quite short, showing how you might use some of the tasks and exercises from Section Two in practice. All highlight issues of literacy and include suggestions for further work. With the exception of *The Pet Cellar*, all the material is currently in print. The material on *The Pet Cellar* has been devised so that it can be used even if you cannot find a copy of the book.

Planning

In order to maximise the flexibility of these projects, I have deliberately not presented them in the format of a scheme of work with lesson plans. Your teaching aims and objectives will change according to the needs of the children you're working with. The material on *Jack and the Beanstalk* and *The Arrival* – at each end of the age range – includes sections which discuss planning.

Age suitability

In each of the projects I have indicated the age range for which the material was devised. In practice, the ideas are more flexible than that. The age range indicated on each project is probably best read as an indication of the youngest age group for which the material would be appropriate. The projects can all easily be adapted for use with older children. I have, for example, not only used much of the material in *Jack and the Beanstalk* with 5 and 6 year olds but also with adults in the early stages of devising a pantomime; and I have used *The Arrival* and *The Fall of Troy* with students in Years 9 and 10 in Secondary Schools as well as with Year 6 Primary. You should find that although the content of *The Dunce*, *The Arrival* and *The Fall of Troy* is best suited for older children, the pedagogy holds good for all age groups and the methodology can easily be adapted.

Illustrations and art work

Most of the projects draw on picture books, though the term does no justice to the fine art work in *Voices in the Park*, *Wolves in the Walls* and *The Arrival*, an award winning graphic novel. I have placed considerable emphasis on writing dialogue in this book, but images are very important in drama. For copyright reasons we cannot reproduce images from most of these books – but they are readily available, and where appropriate I have suggested specific images that might be useful to you. For the same reason I have not referred directly to the stylistic and formal qualities of the art work in these projects; but teachers will undoubtedly find them rich sources of inspiration for art work to complement the drama and literacy activities proposed here.

Terms

A short glossary of drama techniques is provided at the end of this section. It should, however, be stated at this point that the term Forum Theatre is used very loosely – to indicate a collaborative process in which the whole class are invited to contribute suggestions and offer assistance to a small group participating in a dramatic exchange. Thus the improvisation involving as few as two people becomes part of a process of collective playwriting.

Similarly, I have used Dorothy Heathcote's concept of the Mantle of the Expert in the broadest sense: participants taking on a collective role as experts, developing responsibility and ownership of specific material as they do so.

The abbreviation TiR stands for teacher in role.

Years 1 and 2
Jack and the Beanstalk
Approaching, using and developing a traditional story through drama

Enactment of a story
Dialogue and voice
Narrative structure and storyboarding
Point of view
Writing in role
Literacy development

In this project I have assumed a knowledge of the traditional story, although there are several variants.

1. Read and enact the story, breaking it into moments, and encouraging the children to make as many decisions as possible about *how* we are going to represent moments in the story, trying wherever possible to tease out the meanings of these moments.

Examples

Jack leading his mother's cow. How does he do this? It's not easy leading a cow when it doesn't want to move. What else does he take with him when he goes to market?

Jack meeting the stranger with the beans. Constructing teacher in role as the stranger. Exchange between Jack and the bean-seller using Forum Theatre methods – a child as Jack, with the teacher as bean-seller.

Similar exchanges between Jack and his mother, Jack and the giant's wife, in each instance constructing the teacher in the role. What does she feel about what Jack has done? How does she talk? What kind of things does she say?

In developing a moment from the story, in moving from an exchange which is a small part of a larger narrative to something which is a dramatic scene in its own right, consider what each of the characters wants from the given situation; and, if possible, make these wishes conflict. Thus, Jack's Mum might want to sell the cow; Jack might be emotionally attached to it. If there is an element of persuasion in a scene, the content is likely to become more interesting.

2. Read the first part of the story and work with the children to dramatise alternative endings.

This can be especially useful if it is a less well known story that the children have not previously encountered. One of the benefits of this way of working is that it can encourage *active* listening and *active* reading. It stimulates curiosity about the given text.

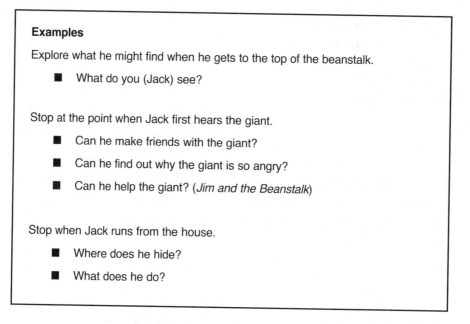

Examples

Explore what he might find when he gets to the top of the beanstalk.

- What do you (Jack) see?

Stop at the point when Jack first hears the giant.

- Can he make friends with the giant?
- Can he find out why the giant is so angry?
- Can he help the giant? (*Jim and the Beanstalk*)

Stop when Jack runs from the house.

- Where does he hide?
- What does he do?

3. Associated characters and their stories

Make a list with the children of all the people who are in any way involved with the story – in this instance, Jack, Jack's mother, the bean-seller, the giant, the giant's wife.

Then make a list of all those minor characters who might appear in the story, or might be connected with it, but aren't usually mentioned:

Examples

- Jack's friends

- Neighbours

- Traders at the market where Jack had been taking the cow

- Jack's teacher

Explore these minor characters through thought-tracking or Forum Theatre:

- Teacher in role as Jack's mother trying to find out what really happened yesterday when Jack was supposed to be taking the cow to market? 'Is there anybody who saw Jack with our cow?'

4. Explore what might have happened before the story starts

Examples

- Jack and his mother living in poverty. What other work have Jack and his mother tried to get them out of poverty?

- Creating the market – what do people sell at markets?

- Creating a wider community around Jack and his mother's house.

- How do other people in the community know Jack and his mother?

- The giant terrorising the people of Jacksville. (There are several versions of the story in which this occurs, thereby justifying Jack's thefts as moral retribution).

- What makes the giant so grumpy?

- Can we find a way of cheering him up? (Perhaps using Forum Theatre, with TiR as the giant)

- Why does the giant eat 'Englishmen' or 'little 'uns'? (depending on which version you're reading!)

- Where does the bean-seller get the magic beans?

- Why is he so keen to exchange them for an old cow that produces very little milk?

5. Explore what's happening elsewhere while the well-known story is taking place

Examples

- Jack's mother searching for her missing son, enlisting the help of neighbours and police.

- A search party organised to climb the beanstalk and find Jack

- Role-play the setting of the story. Create a map of different areas (eg Jack's village, shops, park, houses, market) and explore in role

6. Explore what happens after the story has ended

Examples

- How does Jack spend his new found riches?

- What does the bean-seller do when he hears how Jack has profited from the magic beans?

- Neighbours trying to persuade Jack to let them have a share of the new found wealth

- Making peace with the badly injured giant. Looking after him. Tending to his injuries

- The giant's wife finding a way to get down to Jacksville and seek her injured husband

- Assuming that there are no more magic beans, finding a way of building a tower/ladder big enough to get the giant back up to his home

7. Storyboarding. Re-telling the story through a sequence of still images

Teacher narrates the story. Depending on the age, ability and experience of the children, they either work in small groups and decide on a set of key moments within the story, or the teacher discusses what are the most important moments in the story with the class. Then the children make still images of each of these moments. Once the children have made the still images, the characters in each of the images could be developed through thought tracking. Dialogue could be added. The images could be transferred to a class storyboard and/or comic strip.

8. Using dialogue from the original story

A range of activities – see below.

9. Retelling the story from a different point of view

Examples

Jack's mother

Neighbours

The giant (possibly sad and lonely as in *Jim and the Beanstalk*)

The giant's wife

The bean-seller

10. Taking the story in a different direction

Examples

The giant enters crying because his special pet, the hen, has been taken.

Jack's mother is upset because ever since he got the magic beans, she can't control Jack any more and needs advice ....

Literacy development

Some of the following activities are possible with most of the above approaches; some are only applicable to a few.

Record the dialogue spoken by the characters and written collaboratively with the children. This might include the exchanges that take place within the story, such as Jack's encounters with the bean seller, or beyond the existing story.

Create a storyboard, either directly onto large sheets of paper, or first discussing with the children the most significant moments in the story and then creating still images with the children. The storyboard can be developed into a class comic strip, with dialogue added in speech balloons.

Role on the wall

Draw an outline of any of the characters on a large sheet of paper. Write on the sheet words that describe him/ her. This can be elaborated by writing *outside* the outline those characteristics that are seen by others and *within* the outline the feelings of the character – eg to others the giant is ugly, frightening, loud, large; inside, he may feel lonely, unhappy, hungry.

Making maps

These might be geographical maps or emotional maps – that record in words and pictures the way someone remembers a journey.

- Jack's journey to market, showing where he met the bean-seller
- Where Jack's mother's house is
- The land at the top of the beanstalk

Interviews

These could be undertaken as small group work – the teacher working with a small group – or as a whole group, with the teacher focusing the children's input – a kind of Forum Theatre. Interviews then recorded on video or audio, then transcribed, so the children can see what they have created in written form.

- Police or journalists talking to neighbours and anyone else who saw Jack on the day before his disappearance; talking to Jack's mother

Making posters

A *Missing* poster, made by Jack's mother, or a *Wanted* poster, made by the giant. In both cases this could include a description of Jack as well as a drawing of him.

Secret directions from Jack that he leaves behind (where? – a decision to be made by the children) explaining how to get to the giant's house, and where he will be hiding if anyone comes to rescue him.

Letters – depending on age and ability of children, can be written individually or collectively

- From Jack which he drops from the clouds, explaining what has happened and asking for people to come and rescue him
- From the giant to the people of Jacksville offering them a reward for the return of the bag of gold and the golden hen
- From the people of Jacksville, pleading with the giant to leave them alone

Lists

- Things Jack needs to take with him as he prepares to climb the Beanstalk
- Things Jack's rescuers need to take with them if they are to mount an expedition to find him
- What we will need to help nurse the injured giant back to health
- Shopping list for Jack to take to market

Instructions to leave with the giant for anyone who is tending his injuries

Labels and signs
Making signs to place in the school hall, thereby establishing the fictional geography of the drama

- To the market
- Jacksville
- Names of shops
- Name of giant's house

Newspaper headlines reporting the events in Jacksville – possibly to accompany still images as photographs, or drawings as photographs, or (if you have a digital camera and easy access to a printer) actual photographs of still images which then assume the status of published photographs of the events of the story.

Using dialogue extracts taken from the original story

- Add faces to the dialogue – as a way of attributing character to the lines. Who is speaking? Then names instead of faces. Try it out. How does it sound?

- Add dialogue to the dialogue! Whole class or small group discussion. Two lines of dialogue before and two lines after the given two-line exchange. Children's dialogue written by the teacher on whiteboard so they can see how it looks

- Cut out a selection of the dialogue extracts (in resources below). Mix them up. Ask the children to put them in an order which makes sense, to create a narrative. If this is being done with a story that the children have not yet encountered, it stimulates curiosity about the story

- Create still images to accompany the spoken dialogue – either the simple two-line exchange or the developed six-line scenes

- Bring the still images to life to make short scenes

- Create a sequence with these short scenes – and explore the different ways they tell the story

Resources

The following websites are useful:

University of Southern Mississippi: The *Jack and the Beanstalk* and *Jack the Giant-Killer Project*

http://www.usm.edu/english/fairytales/jack/jackhome.html

British Council/BBC BritLit Primary Kit, *Jack and the Beanstalk*

The aim of BritLit materials is to 'help teachers from around the world to exploit English literature in the ELT classroom as a language tool'. The *Jack and the Beanstalk* material could easily be adapted for use in schools. It aims to 'actively engage children and develop their cognitive, linguistic and social skills.'

http://www.teachingenglish.org.uk/try/resources/britlit/jack-beanstalk

Years 1 and 2
Not Now Bernard
by David McKee

Some possibilities for approaching a well known picture story through drama

Observation
Dialogue and voice
Point of view
Writing in role

The purpose of this project is to explore how some of the ideas developed in *Jack and the Beanstalk* might be adapted for use with a different kind of story. I have not suggested whether it would be best to work in small groups or as a whole class. Both would be possible, though this age group finds it difficult to work at tasks unsupervised. It would, however, be possible to take a small group and work with them while another teacher or assistant worked with the rest of the class.

Enacting the story
Preliminary discussion: look at the pictures and talk about Bernard's family and the house where he lives. What do people do in the house before Bernard finds the monster? What do we know about the house itself?

- Mum and Dad both do DIY: Dad hammers nails into the wall (or tries to), Mum paints walls
- Dad reads the paper
- Mum waters her indoor plants, makes dinner
- Bernard tries to talk to his Mum and Dad but they are always too busy
- The house has a garden, a kitchen and a living room

73

- They have pot plants indoors, and a television
- Bernard has a room with toys and books
- Bernard's bedroom is upstairs

With young children I would usually work in role myself, allowing them to tell me *how* to play the character.

We can start simply by trying out the actions seen in the story. You, the teacher, might say to the class, 'If I'm going to be Bernard's Dad, *how* should I be hammering nails before Bernard comes into the room? Should it be gentle taps, or what? How good is he at DIY? I wonder why he gets so impatient with Bernard?' Try out the different ideas. Do the same with Mum.

The dialogue in *Not Now Bernard* may be minimal, but it can still be used dramatically. *how* should Bernard say 'Hello, Dad' and 'Hello, Mum'? And *how* should his parents reply, '*Not Now Bernard*'? Again, try out the different possibilities.

Children love the repetition of the book, but that in itself allows you to experiment with changing tone, and to introduce vocabulary to describe actions. The approach is similar to that suggested for *Jack and the Beanstalk* – identifying actions, breaking the story into moments, and encouraging the children to think about detail and to make decisions around the enactment of the story.

Take one of the simple exchanges between Bernard and one of his parents, and develop further dialogue. For example, when Mum is watering the house plant in the story she just says '*Not Now Bernard*'. What else might she say?

What other things – in addition to those we see in the book – might Bernard's parents do in a day?

So many children and teachers are familiar with *Not Now Bernard* that it's probably not possible to explore alternative endings in the ways suggested with *Jack and the Beanstalk*. But there is great potential for expanding and developing the story, by considering other characters who might have some connection with the story and what might happen after the story has ended.

Other characters

Collaboratively, make a list of anyone else who might be involved with the story:

Examples

- Bernard's grandparents
- Neighbours
- Bernard's teacher
- Shopkeepers and assistants
- Checkout staff at supermarket

Dramatise an interaction between Bernard, one of his parents and one other person from the list you have made. You might start with an action and one line of dialogue from each of the participants.

Example

In the local shop, Bernard picks up a packet of crisps.

Shopkeeper   Is that everything?

Bernard's Mum   Can I have these?

Mum   Not now, Bernard.

The task seems very simple, but it asks the children to extrapolate from the given story and to consider vocabulary, tone and register, as well as encouraging observation skills.

As in *Jack and the Beanstalk*, when you come to write the dialogue down, you can either attribute speech to named characters or to images of the characters, photocopying from the book or having the children make their own images.

Looking at the story from different perspectives

Most of the children in Years 1 and 2 with whom I have worked on this story see Bernard and the monster as the same person. They enjoy both the metaphor and the metamorphosis. The monster may eat Bernard, but he's not frightened of it, smiling when he sees it. The monster is a dramatically engaging device, enabling us to explore monstrous behaviour through the protection of a fantasy. Drama needs to work in a similar way. Children need the protection and the engagement of an appropriate fictional frame; they need to be caught up in the drama whilst feeling safe within it. That is why it's possible to use a book like *Not Now Bernard* to explore potentially difficult areas. When they move into the world of the drama, they go to a place where they can explore the consequences of decisions they would never make in the real world.

Monster Watch!

Teacher in role as Bernard's Mum or Dad goes to the class and asks them for advice. 'My son has turned into a monster and I don't know what to do.' This is not strictly Mantle of the Expert, but you are endowing the children with the expertise of good parenting.

Using some of the techniques of Forum Theatre, you play out each of the suggestions. As in the enactment work, it's important to seek out the detail, to follow up suggestions with further questions. For example, one of the class suggests that you should listen more carefully to the monster, you might ask, 'How?' 'Show me.' 'If I'm making the tea and he comes in and says, 'Hello Mum', what am I supposed to do?'

And what about Bernard? What should Bernard do to make sure he doesn't get eaten by the monster again?

You might conclude the work by collaboratively writing the letter or e-mail they would like to send to Bernard's parents, explaining to them how to stop Bernard getting eaten by the monster again.

Years 2 and 3
The Pet Cellar
by Michael Bragg

Writing and reading in role

Points of view
Dialogue and voice
Constructing character
Meanings beyond the literal
Emotional maps

About the book

The Pet Cellar is a large format picture book with short narrative sections, some containing dialogue. At the time of writing it is no longer in print, although second hand copies are fairly easy to obtain. I include it here to exemplify some of the ways in which it is possible to introduce a book to children through drama and playwriting; to use the fact that they have no prior knowledge of the book to arouse their curiosity, to stimulate their own stories, dramas and plays. The book has a strong narrative, with mythic qualities. I have used it a great deal with children of all ages, who have always responded to it very positively.

The book opens with a picture of the window of a pet shop. On display in the window are various animals, the kinds that many families have as domestic pets: a puppy, rabbits, guinea-pigs, kittens and cage-birds. All the animals are looking towards the doorway, curious about the two small boys standing there. The written narrative starts:

'That's funny. I haven't seen this shop before,' said Robert...

Leaving his little brother in the doorway, he enters the shop. All is not as he expected. He and the reader enter an *Alice in Wonderland* nightmare world.

There are numerous caged animals, but no human being, until suddenly a frightening looking man appears from behind a cage.

> ''What are you doing?' roared a loud voice... 'I don't like boys, and I don't like boys looking,' snarled Mr Creech, the owner.

Robert turns and runs; but he quickly gets lost and finds himself in a vast network of cages in which there are numerous animals, most of them unlike anything Robert has ever seen before. And Mr Creech is chasing after him. 'Come out boy. I'll find you. Where are you?' Terrified, Robert wanders deeper and deeper into the labyrinthine cellar – until he finds himself in front of a particularly large cage, where an enormous golden bird is imprisoned. He finds himself caught in her gaze and drawn to the cage. Just as the bird pushes a large blue egg towards him, Robert hears Mr Creech roaring from above, 'I'll find you, boy.'

Robert takes the egg and runs on to hide from Mr Creech, who comes chasing after him through the labyrinth of cages and underground passages. With Mr Creech very close behind him, shouting 'You'll never get out of here', Robert nears a set of steps and feels something happening to the egg. 'Just as Mr Creech cried, 'Got you!'... the egg cracked right across....'

A 'magnificent flying creature, just like the one in the cage' emerges from the egg, carries Robert up the steps, out of the shop and to the nearby park, where it sets him down. Robert's little brother joins him; and together they watch the winged creature vanish into the distance.

I suspect that one of the reasons that children respond so positively to *The Pet Cellar* is not only because it has a strong character in the melodramatically villainous Mr Creech and a powerful narrative, but also that the story has such rich mythic connections and resonances – with its echoes of *The Minotaur* and *The Phoenix*.

It is a story that lends itself to interventions. We might, for example:

- stop the narrative at the point where Robert first encounters Mr Creech

- stop at the point where he finds the golden bird

- shift the perspective, so we dramatise the events from the point of view of Robert's brother waiting outside, or those worried about the little boy sitting outside the pet shop.

If you stop at the point where he finds the golden bird, you might encourage the children to speculate about what happens next, and develop drama from those suggestions.

Examples

- Robert imprisoned by Mr Creech and planning his escape
- Robert's brother seeking help from Robert's friends
- Robert escaping from *the Pet Cellar* and organising the rehoming of all the animals

Populating the drama

One of the first things to do when planning any drama is to consider the people in the story. In this instance, the only named characters are Robert and Mr Creech. But the story starts with Robert asking his little brother to wait outside the shop while he goes inside. I usually ask the children to give Robert's brother a name. One class called him Charlie, so that is how I shall refer to him from here on.

THE PET CELLAR
written and illustrated by MICHAEL BRAGG

Methuen Children's Books . London

We might then discuss who else might be involved in the story. The list might include:

- the people working in the bakery next door to the pet shop
- customers in the bakery who saw Robert and Charlie
- the elderly couple looking in the window
- the brothers' parents, grandparents
- Robert's teacher
- Robert's friends, Charlie's friends

- RSPCA officers
- police officers
- traders who have sold Mr Creech the animals
- traders from whom Mr Creech buys his animal feed, bedding and cages
- other customers who have had dealings with Mr Creech

If you have the book to hand, you could use as an initial stimulus the pictures at the frontispiece of the story, where an elderly couple are looking in the *Pet Cellar* window and the next door shop is a bakery.

Intersecting story lines

As discussed in *Structure, Story and Narrative*, we can use the existing story, and consider how other stories might intersect with it. What would happen if ...

- other people came into the shop while Mr Creech was trying to catch Robert in the cellar?
- Charlie came into the shop in search of Robert and overheard Mr Creech shouting?
- Charlie then got a friend to come back with him, and together they went into the shop and tried to persuade Mr Creech to let them look around the cellar?
- Charlie remained on the step outside, too frightened to move?

With this last suggestion, the drama might then begin with a Forum, with you, the teacher, as Charlie and children taking on the roles of various people encouraging him to talk, trying to discover what has happened.

Forum Theatre could also be used with the idea of persuading Mr Creech to allow Charlie and his friend to look around the cellar. In this instance it would be useful to start the Forum with the class constructing the character of Mr Creech. His voice can be heard very clearly in the way he refers to Robert as 'boy': 'I don't like boys, and I don't like boys looking.' 'Come out boy.' 'I'll find you, boy.' You could take on the role of Mr Creech, and ask the children to construct the character, handing responsibility to them, enabling them both to confront their fears, and take control over them. 'I'll play Mr Creech, but you'll have to tell me how to do it...'

- What kinds of things should he say?
- How should he speak? Quiet and threatening? Loud?

■ What words, what phrases? Vocabulary.

■ How does he look? How can I do that?

Ask the children to show you as well as tell you. That not only gets them thinking visually, but gives them a chance to try out ideas in dramatic terms. Ask if you're doing it the way they want you to. When you come to play out the Forum, hold something in reserve. Find a way of challenging them a little further: play the role in the way they have asked you to do it, but add something unexpected. You might let slip that beneath the bluster and the angry voice there is a sad and lonely man whose shop has been regularly broken in to. A class I once worked with on *The Pet Cellar* decided that the drama should be about the rehabilitation of Mr Creech!

Literacy and playwriting activities

Using Forum Theatre techniques to construct the character of Mr Creech and play out the attempt by Charlie and his friend to talk their way past him is itself a form of collaborative playwriting. As you work together you might write on a whiteboard, or ask the class to write, what you decide about Mr Creech. The exchange itself could be recorded and summarised in dialogue form. You might stop the Forum before it reaches a resolution and ask the children individually or in small groups to complete the dialogue.

Other literacy activities that you might use with this material might include:

■ a map of the journey taken by Robert and Charlie from home to pet shop

where do they go?

what and who do they encounter?

how do they feel about these encounters?

This map could be translated into images, a storyboard and/or scenes

■ Robert imprisoned in a cage writing a message (or text on his mobile phone) telling that he has been captured and imprisoned

■ if Robert escapes, writing to the police or RSPCA telling them what he has seen, asking them to do something

■ his letter might then include

a plan of the premises, a map of the area, the park, other shops etc.

a list of animals that Robert saw while he was in the cellar

a description of the pet shop

- if one of the boys is trapped in the cellar, witness statements – who saw Robert/Charlie last? Text messages from witnesses.

Reading in role

Many of these activities ask the class to work in role. How then to feed it back into the fiction? You, the teacher, might read it in role. In the case of some of the work suggested above you might respond to it by:

- telephoning a squad car and get them to call on Mr Creech

- gathering RSPCA officers around (children as experts), deciding whether to act on Robert's letter, devising a plan to rescue the animals

- using Robert's letter as evidence, one or more of the children in the class has to persuade you, the teacher (as police officer or RSPCA officer) to conduct an investigation

Working on *The Pet Cellar* with children I have often found that what has started as an exciting and scary fantasy has evolved into a serious investigation into the problems of releasing caged animals back into the wild.

Years 2 and 3
Voices in the Park
by Anthony Browne

Points of view
Dialogue
The concept of voice
Metaphor and symbol
Observation
Character
Narrative structure

About the book

Voices in the Park shows us the same events from four different points of view. The story line seems very simple: two families – mother and son from a wealthy family, out-of-work father and daughter – take their dogs for a walk in the park. The mother and father have no contact with each other, but the dogs and the children play with each other and quietly defy social expectations. The book is deeply humane in its exploration of the power of friendship in overcoming snobbery and social prejudice, and wonderfully rich visually. One of the great pleasures in the book is looking closely at the illustrations. When Charles and his mother go to the park, for example, the shadow of one of the trees seems to be a crocodile and one of the others casts a shadow as if it were on fire. At the end, as they walk out of the park gates, we can see a tree on fire. Nobody seems to have noticed. Children enjoy looking carefully at the illustrations, picking up on what the characters seem to miss. The effect is to empower the viewer, but also to draw attention in a wry and humorous way to our different perceptions of events. Children find the strangeness of the pictures provocative and stimulating.

In keeping with much of Anthony Browne's work, his humans are depicted as apes – a strategy that echoes the need in drama to engage children in deep and challenging issues whilst simultaneously protecting them from potentially damaging self-exposure.

Characters

Discuss and list what we know about each of the characters in the book, starting with 'Who is telling each story?'

1) Mother
2) Dad
3) Charles
4) Smudge

What else do we know about each of these four?

How do they talk? What kind of vocabulary do they use? What kind of accent do you think they have?

What are the names of the dogs? (Victoria and Albert (!), though Smudge's Dad refers to Albert as 'the dog' when he is speaking.) How do you think each character calls the dog when they're out? How do you think each character calls the dog when they're out? How do they talk to the dog? And what does the way they talk to their dog reveal about them as characters?

Identifying voices

Starting with what appears in the book itself, choose two to four sentences from each of the four voices which identify the voice of the characters through the way that they speak.

First Voice
You get some frightful types in the park these days!
'Charles, come here. At once!'

Second Voice
Me and Smudge took the dog to the park.
You've got to have some hope, haven't you?

Third Voice
It's so boring. Mummy said it was time for our walk.
I'm good at climbing trees, so I showed her how ...
Mummy caught us talking...

Fourth Voice
He went straight up to this nice dog and sniffed its bum (he always does that).
I thought he was kind of a wimp at first, but he's okay.

Who's who in tabular form

Voice	Whose voice?	Characteristics	Vocabulary	Accent
First	Mother			
Second	Dad			
Third	Charles, the son			
Fourth	Smudge, the daughter			

Dog	Characteristics
Victoria	
Albert	

In many of the projects in this section, I have suggested that it's useful to start your planning for drama by thinking about *who*, in addition to the named characters in the original story, might be involved. In this instance, where the focus is on point of view and differing perspectives, the four given characters give us plenty of material, especially if we use the story as a starting point from which to speculate about the characters and their lives.

Consider, for example, each of the families at home.

■ How do the adults organise the space? If, for example, Mummy, is very controlling, how does this manifest itself in terms of what she says to Charles and asks him to do?

■ What are mealtimes like in each home?

■ What do they have for tea?

■ When do they eat?

■ Where do they eat?

■ How are meals served?

■ Where is the dog while the 'humans' are eating?

After discussion, small groups might dramatise a mealtime. In order to prevent rambling, shapeless improvisations, the task is better undertaken with constraints – perhaps starting with a clear task – such as making a still image to show where in the house the meal takes place (watching TV, kitchen, dining room) and where the dog is in relation to adult and child. Limited dialogue can be added, perhaps two lines to start with, developed into eight.

From this you might discuss and then dramatise other aspects of the ways in which the adults and children interact:

- What happens at bedtime?
- How do each of the parents tell the child it is bed time?
- Where does the dog sleep?

- Mummy's hopes for Charles. How does she talk about this with him?
- Dad's hopes for Smudge.

- How do each of the adults respond when the child comes home from school with something important to tell them?

- How does each of the four characters express emotion? What language do they use to say that they feel happy, disappointed, worried, excited?

Further development in related areas

Tell the children an everyday story which lends itself to being seen from different points of view.

Example:

Yesterday, our student teacher came back into the classroom after lunch with tomato ketchup stains all down the front of his shirt, and he didn't know about it. It was really funny. I didn't see it at first, but my friend told me and then I saw it. I tried really hard to stop myself from laughing. Then someone told the student and everyone started laughing. He looked really cross at first, then even he laughed at himself.

Discuss, and then make a list of the different people who might in some way have been connected with this story, for example:

- the student teacher
- the class teacher
- the headteacher
- a dinner lady
- a parent visiting the school for the first time
- a child who doesn't like the student teacher
- a child who does like the student teacher

Discuss:

- What would each person think and feel about the situation?

- What might each person particularly remember about this story?
- What different kinds of words would they use, how would their voice change depending on their point of view?

If you were leading the discussion with the whole class, then you might write suggestions on the whiteboard or flip chart; with a more experienced class, you might put them into small groups, assign each group one of the characters associated with the story and give them a printed table, similar to the one used with *Voices in the Park*, for them to work with.

As a whole class or in small groups, they then re-write the story according to each of the different points of view.

Each group shares their version of the story.

Make a five frame storyboard, or series of five still images, telling the story of the spilt ketchup from their character's point of view.

Class to suggest other simple stories that can be told from different points of view, and might be undertaken in conjunction with work on observation (see pp55-61).

Years 3 and 4
The Kraken

An account of a process drama with a Year 4 class

Extensive cross-curricular work
Writing and reading in role
Narrative structure
Metaphors, symbols

Introduction and Context

This is an account of an extended process drama project with links across many curriculum areas. The project comprised a series of six drama lessons that took place in the school hall over seven weeks with one Year 4 class. During this time the children also undertook several hours of related work (including research, writing in role, playwriting and art work) in the classroom.

This process drama approach, in which the teacher allows the drama to become a motivating force at the centre of the curriculum, can be very rewarding. But it requires opportunities to use time flexibly and demands that the teacher is as alert to the social and learning needs of the children as she is to the drama. I am not recommending that you leave the delivery of the National Curriculum to chance and vaguely hope that drama will lead you into appropriate areas. But I am convinced that lively interaction between different subject areas is at the heart of this kind of drama; that this kind of process engages children, stimulates highly motivated creative and imaginative learning, and is profoundly enriching.

In this particular drama a strong narrative line develops. This was not imposed by the teacher but derives from the particular type of questions asked. These questions are highlighted in bold in the documentation. If you want to follow the model, I suggest that you use the introductory activities, the strategies, the starting point and similar questions, but be wary of using the story line itself as a model. The children in this class were hooked by it because they felt a strong sense of ownership both for the story and for the material it generates. The danger of using the material as it is presented here without modification is that children who had not been party to the creation and development of the story might be baffled and bored by it.

Format
Text on the left of the page is descriptive; on the right is comment and analysis.

Background information
I was working in the school as part of a continuing CPD project. I led the drama workshops; the class teacher and I collaborated on the planning. In the account of the project below I refer to myself as the teacher.

School and catchment: urban, with largely working class catchment area.

Class: 32 children. Many are from single parent families. Few have had any experience of being read to at home. No previous experience of drama in the school.

The aims of the drama are:

- to develop oral language and vocabulary amongst the children
- to develop their understanding of narrative
- to develop their understanding of meaning beyond the literal
- to motivate a range of cross curricular work and to explore the links between different curriculum areas.

The Drama
Twilighting
The drama begins with an exercise in which the children make still images of monsters, first on their own and then in pairs. How do these monsters feed and move? We look at a few examples. Audience asked to think of appropriate names for these creatures and to suggest an appropriate habitat for them. They make sound pictures using voices, musical instruments and other found items (for example torn newspaper) to create the atmosphere of the habitat. Two creatures which particularly interest the children are named a Dragosaurus and a Kraken.

> I am sure they chose Kraken because it had appeared in a film recently shown on television. The teacher accepts the idea but explains to the children that any drama

which involves a Kraken will not be a dramatisation of the story they already knew. 'It will be our own story about a Kraken.'

'Now we're going to make a play. In the play there will be a Kraken. I don't know when it will appear. That's part of the mystery. I think it'll be more exciting if we don't know quite when we we're going to meet it.'

This strategy creates dramatic tension before the drama has even started. They know that something is going to happen, but not when or how. At a later stage, it will be useful to reflect on this with the children as a structural principle of story telling and play making, relating it to other stories that they know.

'Our drama will take place in a village. The people who live in it have no electricity, no gas, no cars. I wonder how they get their food, how they cook their food?'

The teacher sets the scene and establishes the parameters. The reason for setting the drama in a fictional past is in order to encourage the establishment of an interdependent community, in which each person's actions affect others. In strictly historical terms this may be a romantic or even nostalgic notion; but it enables the children to work together as a team and facilitates the development of a cause and effect narrative.

Preliminary discussion of the kinds of activities that would take place in such a village, asking children to make suggestions and then enabling them to research their ideas.

For this kind of relatively open ended process drama to motivate and drive cross curricular work, the teacher has to provide good quality materials that the children can use for their own research.

Small group improvisations, moving into whole group work

The teacher puts the children into small groups, in each of which they work through a simple improvisation (based on earlier discussion and research) showing how they get food. This leads to further discussion. During this, and with the teacher's assistance, they allocate roles to themselves: farmers, millers, hunters, fishermen, pot makers, net menders, woodcutters etc.

During the discussion it is also decided that the village is on the outer edge of a forest, which surrounds a large lake.

Key questions posed at this stage include:

'If the people want to have a meeting, where do they meet?'
The children decide it should be the market place.

'What is there to mark this meeting place?'

A large wooden cross.

> I suspect the children suggested this because they had encountered crosses as markers in stories and films as well as in the Christian story. As with the Kraken, it is important to accept the suggestion and then to work with it, helping the children to explore its meanings to this community. Given the specific aims of this drama and the importance of enabling children to explore meanings beyond the literal, it is important to remain alert to the rich symbolic possibilities of the image.

'How can we make that cross in the hall? What can we use to represent that cross?'

The children decide to use one of the benches in the hall. This is stood up and leant against the wall.

> Note that this question is out of role. It is a question about a formal issue of representation and signification. The children have no problems moving in and out of role. As yet the teacher has not taken on a role within the drama.

'Why does it not have a cross piece?'

> The question accepts the children's suggestion, but aims to develop its significance. Questioning should never deny what the children have offered, but aim to develop and deepen meaning. Instead of saying, 'We'll make do with the bench' the absence of a cross piece is itself given significance. This question encourages the children to work *with* their chosen object, encourages them to continue to seek meanings with rich metaphorical and symbolic potential. By asking an open question, the teacher is also communicating to the children not only that they are contributing actively to the development of the drama, but that the teacher does not have all the answers in this process; that this drama will be a collaborative process in which every participant will have the power to affect the narrative and to tease out its meanings.

The children decide that it is very old, and that the cross piece fell off many years ago.

'Is there anything particularly special about this cross?'

There's a legend that if anyone touches it, a Kraken will be awakened from the depths of the lake.

> This could have been a good point at which to discuss out of role what they, the children as makers of the drama, not in role as the villagers, wanted and expected the *Kraken* to be. With younger children, it would be important to ask whether they wanted it to be frightening, giving them control of their own fear. In this instance, where the drama could evolve over several weeks, I thought it better to assess their needs through their responses to the drama itself.

Symbolism

This image, the representation of the cross in the hall, proves very potent. In the following week the drama begins with erecting the cross. Later, the children build their own out of cardboard boxes stuck together, painting it to look as if it were wood.

The cross is a powerful and central symbol in the Christian religion; a symbol of suffering, persecution, redemption and salvation. Whilst it's important to acknowledge and respect the different cultural reference points that each child brings to the interpretation of symbol and metaphor, our drama is not a retelling of the Christian story. And we are not appropriating a Christian symbol.

At this stage in the drama, the cross functions as little more than a marker for the village meeting place; but that is important in itself. It is already a sign that can be read at several levels. Within the fiction of the drama it is a sign that this is a place where everybody's voice can be heard as the villagers meet to discuss issues which concern them. It simultaneously has an important function within the social environment of the school. It provides a clear focus for the children, it raises the seriousness of the drama and it enhances the children's sense of ownership of their work. The act of erecting the bench each time we enter the school hall for drama becomes a formal sign that the nature of the space is being changed.

An image like this has the potential to be a rich symbol. Even though the children themselves suggested it, it is only through the drama, through their interaction with it, that the breadth and depths of its meanings are created. Symbols do not spring into life on their own; they are a product of social and cultural usage. Drama reflects that, and the gradual evolution of the complexity of the cross symbol in this particular drama is a clear demonstration that children can develop a sophisticated grasp of the concept of non-literal meaning at an early age. As Tag McEntagart has noted, children's 'strongest wish and uppermost impulse is to want to make sense of ... meaning for themselves.' (1981:48)

At the end of each week's drama in the hall, and in periods of reflection during the hall time, it was possible to speak of the symbolic significance of the cross. This was done through observations, questions, discussions and the children's own written work. The questions included those which are best described as 'wondering questions'; questions to which there may not be immediate answers but which encourage a spirit of curiosity. In this instance, some such questions included:

- I wonder why the villagers have chosen to keep this cross to mark their meeting place? Why they have not made a new one?

- I wonder what gave rise to that legend about the Kraken?

- I wonder whether all the villagers believe the legend?

Wondering sows seeds, encourages the children to take their own ideas seriously.

Map making

'If the cross is in the meeting place and the lake's over here, where's the mill?'
In class time, a map of the village is made, showing the lake, the forest, the meeting place and all the places which have been mentioned in drama time. The small groups in which the children have been working in the hall make pictures of their area. On a large roll of paper, the teacher draws a representation of the lake and the river. After a discussion of the concept of scale, time and distance, the children place their pictures onto the outline map.

> The making of the map has been engaging in itself. It keeps the children actively engaged in the drama. It begins to make the fictional world more concrete for them.

Reading in role

When we next go to the hall, we take the map with us. The hall space is marked out to reflect the positioning of the different work areas – the mill, the fishing people, the woodcutters etc – as they appear on the map.

> The map making activity is a kind of writing in role. And just as it's vital to value contributions to discussion, it's important to give space for written work to feed back into the drama, for the children to see what they have done as significant, for it to be honoured within the world of the drama. The teacher then has to think how to create opportunities for the map to gather meaning in the fiction. What they have written in role needs to be read in role.

Discussions about the use of the map: Where is it to be stored? Who has access to it?

> Essentially the discussion is opening up the question of how we use the map. But 'Who has access to it?' also provokes thoughts about issues of social organisation.

The children move into what Dorothy Heathcote has referred to as 'busy time'. They play enthusiastically, albeit in rather unfocused fashion, at the roles they have adopted.

Introduction of teacher in role

The teacher asks them all to sit away from the agreed meeting place by the cross; and explains that he will now himself be taking a part in the drama.

> If the children are familiar with the strategy of teacher-in-role, it's not usually necessary to forewarn them. But these children had not worked with a teacher in role before.

The teacher enters in role, moving from group to group, asking what each group is doing and seeking shelter for the night. He is a stranger to the community, claiming to be a carpenter. The villagers do not trust him.

The villagers' mistrust of the stranger came from signals given by the teacher. But it is also an intuitive response on the part of the children, who understand that if he is dangerous in some way it is likely to raise dramatic tension. It's important to recognise this and find time to reflect on it at a later stage (probably at the conclusion of the project) – asking questions along the lines of, 'Do you remember when the stranger first arrived in the village? What was exciting about that?'

Process drama may evolve through collaborative work, but the principles of narrative structure are just as applicable as in any other kind of play making process.

The stranger/carpenter offers to help them and says he is looking for work. He notices the cross, and say that he could repair it for them if they would like him to. Teacher comes out of role and helps them set up a meeting. They can ask the carpenter questions, but only three from each group.

The children accept easily that the teacher can be the carpenter and talk, out of role, about the carpenter as if he were someone else. The strict limitation to the number of questions encourages the groups to give careful thought to the questions they will ask.

The children agree to let the carpenter stay in the village if he will help them repair their boats, but he must not go near the cross.

Writing in role

Out of role, the teacher asks the children about the carpenter:

'I wonder what the villagers think about the carpenter? Who do you think he is? What have you noticed about him? Why do you think he has come here? I wonder what each of the villagers is thinking privately?'

In role, the children write their private thoughts about the carpenter in a diary. In pairs, they whisper their stories to each other.

Out of role, the teacher wonders what might happen if the carpenter were to read some of these. How could that happen? A girl suggests that she can act as a spy. If they deliberately leave some of the diary entries in the house where the carpenter is staying, she can spy on him and watch his reactions.

The teacher reads some of the diary entries in role as the carpenter. The spy watches and reports back to the villagers at a formal meeting.

This exemplifies the concept of reading in role. The written work is valued and given high significance within the fiction of the drama. Children see their written work affecting a character in the drama. The set up of the spying (and the meeting when the observations are reported and discussed) demonstrates the sophistication of which children are capable in drama, having no problems in switching between being in and out of role.

They all watch, out of role, as the girl spies on the carpenter reading the diary entries; and then attend to her report at the subsequent meeting as if they knew nothing of what she had seen.

Research work

Away from the hall they were also busy, working individually and in small groups, undertaking research on a chosen area.

> One child, who had taken on the role of the miller in the village community, finds a fact sheet about water mills in the school library. His water mill has really begun to matter to him. His access to facts, and the mill becoming more real as a result – not only for him, but for all the children – makes the water mill a focus of activity for all the children. It's an interesting example of the potential of this method of working for enhancing commitment to both drama and related curriculum work.

The *Kraken* surfaces

One of the stories told by the children in between drama sessions suggests that the carpenter himself is the Kraken, that the monster can change shapes. They become fascinated by the idea of a Shape Changer. It's an idea borrowed from science fiction but, in the context of this drama, highly relevant. A discussion ensues – out of role.

'How can you find out if the carpenter is a Shape Changer?'

Discussion in small groups and practising

Small groups make plans – taken to a meeting, with one person in each group outlining the group's plans (some accompanied by diagrams). Each group then has an opportunity to practise their idea amongst themselves, with one of them pretending to be the carpenter. They share their ideas again with the whole group and make a decision.

The agreed plan is then carried out, this time with the teacher as the carpenter. The plan is based on the group's assertion that a Shape Changer cannot stop himself reverting to being a Kraken if he is in contact with water. The teacher asks them:

'Do you want the carpenter to be a Shape Changer, a Kraken, or would you rather not know just yet? Would you like to find out when they try out their plan?'

> The class were unanimous in wanting *not* to know until they tried out their plan. Had they wanted the carpenter to be the Kraken in disguise, I might have asked them *how* they wanted me to play the Kraken. This strategy is a kind of Forum Theatre, in which the children construct the teacher in the role.

The plan is put into action: one of the villagers brings some water to the carpenter, who looks very wary. Dramatic tension building up! 'You're not trying to poison me, are you?' 'No'. The carpenter drinks the water and washes in it (mimed). This should show that he is what he says he is, but not all the villagers are convinced. One child gets a jug of water (still mimed) and throws it over the carpenter.

> The child who throws the jug of water was probably fooling around; he was not very engaged in the drama and it's likely he was seeing what he could get away with. Seizing on this as an opportunity, however, the teacher makes it into a significant moment, giving the action meaning beyond that intended by the child, but not denying the action..

The carpenter goes to the villagers in the market place; he tells them: 'I fear I am not welcome. There are many people here who don't want a stranger in their midst. I can understand that; but can I please spend one more night resting in your village? I'll move on in the morning.'

The children/villagers are split now – unsure of their feelings towards the carpenter, unsure of what he represents. Many would like to trust him; some fierce arguments (in role) begin. Persuading, negotiating, compromising way beyond the expectations of the class teacher – and, indeed, the National Curriculum.

Out of role discussion of the narrative. *Dramatic tension*.
At this point the teacher comes out of role and again asks them what they (as children) would like to happen that night – not *how* it would happen nor what it would lead to, nor how the story would end.

> Asking questions about what the children would like to happen should be done in a way that does not reduce the dramatic tension. There are frequent occasions in movies when we have a pretty good idea of what's likely to happen next – it's how it happens that keeps us guessing, keeps us hooked. So too with dramatic tension in a drama lesson.

The children say they want the carpenter to go to the cross in the middle of the night, many of them thinking, even now that this will either turn him into a Kraken, or bring the Kraken from the lake. This is what they really want. The teacher says, 'By tomorrow, I promise you, the villagers will know about the Kraken.'

Teacher as narrator
Children to go to the edge of the hall and close their eyes. Teacher narrates:

'That night, while everybody was asleep, the carpenter went to look at the cross in the market place. He was about to touch it when it fell on him, pinning him down and breaking his legs.'

The teacher lowers the cross, then lies underneath it.

'He cannot move. His cries for help disturb the villagers, who wake and head for the market place.'

Teacher now addresses the children in role, carpenter to villagers:

'You've been suspicious of me since I arrived. And I have a confession to make to you. I fled from my own village on the other side of the lake, where almost all the inhabitants have died of a plague. It is as if they had been poisoned; I fear it is something in the lake. I didn't tell you before because I was terrified that you would send me on my way, that you wouldn't want someone in your village who could be a plague carrier.'

> This intervention raises the stakes of the drama through introducing a threat to the community whilst working within the terms of the fiction that has been developed collaboratively.

The villagers assume that the something is the Kraken. But whatever the Kraken is, it's not visible, perhaps too small to see. One child suggests that the Kraken might be 'a baby bacteria'. She has clearly heard the word in use, but not understood what bacteria are. Another suggests that if it's a baby now it could grow into something huge, 'bigger than the Loch Ness Monster'.

> Authenticity is exciting for children, they have an appetite for it which drama can not only feed but encourage. In drama we should, however, never allow factual information to intimidate them. We should instead create opportunities which encourage them to seek authenticity. A child who actively seeks information, who finds out for herself that bacteria multiply in numbers but don't grow in size will own that knowledge, will feel pride in her achievements in making the discovery. She is also likely to make far better use of the knowledge than children who passively receive the same information as a chore and are constantly reminded how little they know.
>
> This is not to deny that accuracy is important. It matters that a child doesn't leave a drama lesson believing that bacteria grow into something resembling the Loch Ness Monster, but it is important to find the right moment to correct her, and better still that she discovers the information for herself and proudly shares it with the class.

The drama continues for several weeks. In the classroom, water tests are devised, the use of magnifying glasses and microscopes introduced. After heated discussion the children decide that the Kraken is a sort of bacteria.

Although most of them have heard of bacteria, they have no idea what they actually are; this adds to the excitement and sense of discovery. Their plague/Kraken protection measures begin with a decision to sieve their drinking water! Gradually, as research and drama work grow together, some of the abler children develop a remarkably sophisticated understanding of micro-organisms. And in the meantime, in the drama, the miller and his crew divert another river to create an alternative water supply, while the carpenter is nursed back to health (on a diet of herbs) and then enlisted on a programme of public works.

> It is, of course, easy to write that they 'divert a river....' In practice this entails discussion both in and out of role about the pros and cons of diverting the river, who would do the work and, if dams were going to be built, whose trees would be cut down; about how people could divert a river without power machinery – another research task. The busy time work in the hall, miming cutting down trees, for example, is important and enjoyable for the children; but learning from the drama is more likely to take place during interpersonal transactions and interactions – so in this instance it was good that a teaching assistant took on the role of someone on whose land the trees for the dam were to be found.

> It's never easy to know when a drama like this has finished. In this instance, although it would have been possible to develop the drama further, this is where we stop: the problems posed by the arrival of the stranger and the emergence of the *Kraken*, seem to have been solved. The project has, however, taught the children, amongst many other things, that solving one problem often throws up another. It is important to conclude the work with a strong visual image.

The symbol of the cross

We end the drama by talking about the importance of the cross in the lives of the village community; what it meant for the people of the village, what it represented at the beginning of the drama and at the end.

In role, the teacher says, 'I know how important your cross is for you. And I have damaged it. I am a carpenter. Do you want me to help you mend it and set it back up as it used to be?' The responses to this open up a discussion which continues out of role in the classroom, one child suggesting, 'That was the way things used to be,' in effect describing the power of an old order in decay. They agree that they want something different to mark their meeting place, and agreed that instead of a cross they will make a new building in which they can have their meetings in future.

> They have begun to see the cross as a symbol with meanings that none of us could ever have imagined when we embarked on the project. It has become an active image, one that cannot be tied down to specific meanings.

Literacy

The project created opportunities for the children to improve in many areas of literacy. These included:

- listening and retelling stories, using a range of different registers
- speaking formally in role in the public meetings – developing arguments, persuading, negotiating, compromising
- asking relevant questions in appropriate registers
- planning and predicting
- speculating and testing, making informed guesses about possibilities
- oral and written descriptions of events within the fiction
- engaging actively in extensive group discussions – both in and out of role – honouring the contributions of others
- creating and sustaining roles

Their research, which took them to a wide range of print and ICT-based texts, involved:

- investigating, selecting and sorting material
- sharing their research discoveries (in and out of role) through written work, sketches, diagrams and reports

In addition, they also undertook highly motivated work in a wide range of curriculum areas. These included:

Subject area	Examples of work
Geography/Maths:	Map making: scales, measuring time and distance
Technology/Art	Making and painting the cross
	Building a model of the village and the watermill
Science	Research and experimentation into levers, gears and the hardness of materials
	Research into filtering water and the nature of germs, bacteria and micro-organisms
History	Creating time lines and developing understanding of chronology and the concept of cause and effect
	Developing understanding of pre-industrial societies

Subject area	Examples of work
Religious and moral education	Developing understanding of concepts of social interdependence and social responsibility
	Exploration of concepts of justice
	Ritual and symbol
	Exploring moral dilemmas about caring for the sick

Above all, however, the children were motivated to learn; they acquired new interests as well as key skills; they enjoyed their learning. They saw what they were doing not as work, but as pleasure.

Years 4 and 5
Wolves in the Walls
by Neil Gaiman and Dave Mckean

Writing/Reading in role
Using dialogue extracts
Narrative structure
Emotional maps
Point of view

This chapter is intended more as a sketch of possible work than a detailed account.

The book

Lucy, the central character in *Wolves in the Walls*, is convinced there are wolves in the walls of her house. But nobody believes her and, as everybody tells her, 'If the wolves come out of the walls, then it's all over'. Then one day the wolves do come out, and the family flee in panic. But it's not all over for Lucy, who overcomes her fear of the wolves and eventually leads her family back into their house.

Wolves in the Walls is an inventive, witty story, with pictures that blend paint, collage, drawing and photography. It draws on many well known classic children's fictions whilst never imitating them. It's a book about overcoming fears, about resilience and loyalty.

The following material is divided into three sections:

- before reading the book

- during a reading of the book

- work with groups that know the book

Before reading the story
Camouflaging dialogue
After sufficient demonstration in which the class work collectively to develop a short scene around two given lines, divide into small groups.

Small group task. Give out short snippets of dialogue extracted from the book and ask each group to develop short scenes which include these extracts. (See chapter *Dialogue and Voice* for a detailed description of the exercise.) Suggested extracts from *Wolves in the Walls* appear at the end of this chapter.

Audience tries to distinguish between the given lines and those lines written by the groups.

Use the scenes that they have developed to speculate about the story, considering

- Content. What's it about?
- Narrative structure. How does the story begin and end?
- Characters. Who is involved? Who is talking in each of these scenes?
- Genre. What kind of story do you think it will be?

Used like this, the exercise encourages active imagination and intelligent speculation about content; it provokes curiosity about the text. It would be possible to develop some of the stories the groups propose, creating their own versions of *Wolves in the Walls*.

You might ask the groups to consider whether any of the scenes they have watched might go together and if so, how? What order would they go in? If you get two or three which work together, do they need another scene to complete the play? Can they write/improvise that scene? If appropriate, you might give the groups, or the whole class, copies of illustrations from the book to see if they can fit these into their storyboards.

You might discuss the playful use of figurative language – 'It's all over' – and ask groups to include more in their own scenes.

Storyboarding
Give groups a cut up storyboard of pictures with dialogue from the book and ask them to put them in an order which makes sense. Note that you're not asking them to get the right order, but to create an order which makes sense. The feedback and reflection on their work should draw attention to cause and effect in narrative, teasing out the ways that changing the order of events changes the meaning of a story.

With the dialogue and the storyboarding exercises, it is important that when the group encounter the book you don't allow this to become a way of checking who was right in their speculation about it.

During a reading of the book

Read the story aloud, but stop at cliff-hanger points. There are numerous points in the book where you can do this. At any of these points you might ask the class what they think happens next, then try out the ideas. This might result in an extended drama or a short exercise. The following are not prescriptive, but examples of how you might encourage a class to interact with the text in this way.

1. Nobody believes Lucy when she says she can hear noises in the walls. She has to go to bed. Then Lucy says 'I don't like it', to her pig puppet. 'It's too quiet.'

    ■ What might Lucy write in her diary before she goes to sleep? What happens if her Mum then finds the diary?

    ■ What might Lucy write in a text to her best friend? How will her friend react?

    ■ What do you think her parents are saying to each other downstairs while Lucy is in bed? Write just two lines of dialogue.

2. Lucy and her family are at the bottom of the garden. Lucy is worried about her puppet: 'It was chilly at the bottom of the garden... She'll be all alone in that house with the wolves...'

    ■ Lucy makes a plan to go back into the house and leaves a note for her parents to say what she is planning to do

    ■ Lucy tries to persuade her brother to go with her. Her brother finds reasons not to

    ■ Collaborative play writing through Forum Theatre with the teacher as one of the wolves. 'How scary do you want the wolves to be?' 'What is the wolf frightened of?'

3. Lucy has crept back into the house, and found a 'huge wolf ... asleep on her bed ... snoring very loudly. She finds the pig-puppet. 'I was worried sick about you!' she told her pig-puppet...

    ■ The wolves capture Lucy and write a ransom note

    ■ Lucy trapped in the house, writes a note – asking for help or explaining how she might be rescued

■ The wolf on Lucy's bed wakes up. Exchange played out through Forum Theatre – a volunteer as Lucy, the teacher as the wolf

After reading the whole story
Remembering and reflecting on the story

In small groups, make a series of still images which highlight the main points of the narrative. Add two lines of dialogue to each. Dialogue can be taken from the book. Create a storyboard with captions for the images.

Make a plan of the house. What happens in which room? Mark this with dialogue rather than description. These plans might be made by placing individual children's art work in the hall to indicate space – if the kitchen is here, where does Dad practice the tuba? Is it possible to make a plan of the space between the walls?

A map of the house in relation to the neighbourhood – where is the school? Where do Lucy's friends live? Who does Lucy meet in these places?

Making an *emotional map* of Lucy's journeys to and from school, her grandparents' house, her friends' houses, the shops – thus making Lucy a deeper character.

Develop some of the other characters in the story – using role on the wall, Forum Theatre techniques or the adapted *observation questionnaire* provided below.

Rework the story from other points of view:

■ how would Lucy's brother tell the story to his friends?
■ what would the key events in the story be for Lucy's Mum and Dad?
■ how would the wolves remember their stay in the house?

Further Resources

The National Theatre of Scotland produced an adaptation of *Wolves in the Walls* in collaboration with Improbable Theatre.

Learning resources developed to accompany that production can be found on the National Theatre of Scotland website:
http://www.nationaltheatreofscotland.co.uk

> Previous Shows > The *Wolves in the Walls* > Learning Materials

Resources for use in playwriting/drama work on *Wolves in the Walls*
The following dialogue extracts are taken from the book

A Who says that?
B People. Everybody. You know.

A And how does he know?
B Everybody knows

A Whose idea was this anyway?
B Not mine

A If the wolves come out of the walls, then it's all over
B What's all over?

A Who says?
B Mr Wilson at my school

A We could go back and live in our own house
B What about the wolves?

A I don't like it
B It's too quiet

A There are wolves in the walls, Dad
B I don't think there are, poppet

A We could live in a hot air balloon
B We could live in a tree house

A I've left my pig puppet behind
B We can get you a new one

An example of a table of questions to develop an invented character based on a book

Questions	Responses
What is the name of the person you want to write about in your play?	LUCY
A possession or item of clothing that you associate with this person	The pig puppet
Three short statements about him or her based on what you know from the book	She's had the puppet since she was a baby Her Dad plays the tuba Her Mum makes jam
A sound that you associate with this person – but not something s/he says	Noises from the walls – hustling, bustling, crinkling, crackling noises
Something s/he says	'There are wolves in the walls'
A time of day	Late at night
An object or item of furniture that you might associate with this person	Her bed
What does s/he want?	To tame the wolves in the walls.
A fear that s/he *is* willing to admit to other people	That the wolves might do dreadful things to her puppet
A fear that s/he *is* not willing to admit to other people	That *she* herself might be alone in the house with wolves
Imagine this person talking to someone s/he doesn't speak to in the book	
Who is s/he talking to?	Sharon, her best friend at school
Where are they talking?	At Lucy's home in her bedroom
Something you might *imagine* this person saying, that she *doesn't* actually say in the book	Can you hear that?
And what does the other person reply?	What is it?

A copy of this questionnaire for photocopying – with the responses column left empty – can be found in the Resources Section below, p192.

Years 5, 6 and above
The Dunce (Le cancre)
by Jacques Prévert

Detailed accounts of several different ways of using a poem with children

Suggestions for further work
Workshop with student teachers

Enactment of a poem
Use of metaphor and symbol
Writing/Reading in role
Points of view
Dialogue and voice
Character
Observation

The Dunce (Le cancre)
by Jacques Prévert
translated by Lawrence Ferlinghetti

*He says no with his head
but he says yes with his heart
he says yes to what he loves
he says no to the teacher
he stands
he is questioned
and all the problems are posed*

*Sudden laughter seizes him
and he erases all
the words and figures
names and dates
sentences and snares
and despite the teacher's threats
to the jeers of infant prodigies
with chalk of every colour
on the blackboard of misfortune
he draws the face of happiness.*

The Dunce was first published in 1946 in Prévert's collection of poems, *Paroles*. Although adults are sometimes puzzled by the poem, in my experience children usually respond to it very positively. Many need to have the words 'prodigies' and 'snares' explained, but the difficulty posed by the poem lies not in its vocabulary, which is simple, but in its alternation between concrete imagery and metaphor. Indeed, it's this shift that makes it so rich, both as a poem and as a stimulus for drama and dramatic writing.

The first part of this project is based on workshops undertaken with classes of Year 5 and 6 children; the second part offers suggestions for further work with children; the third part describes how I have adapted the material for use in workshops with student teachers as a way of exploring issues around dealing with children who present as isolates or with behavioural problems.

On one occasion, a student teacher said to me that she thought this material was 'anti-school' and 'anti-education'; and that it was risky to use it with children because it could provoke rebelliousness. The poem critiques repressive education paradigms, but children are deeply interested in issues of fairness. The poem and, hopefully, the drama workshops are enabling because they champion resilience and the ability to resist group pressure. The approach suggested here allows and encourages diversity of response, giving children opportunities not only to voice their concerns about bullying, but also to explore notions of fairness and justice. It is only anti-school if school permits the kind of behaviour alluded to in the poem, if the school is structured on the repressive pedagogical model implied by the poem, where what the child loves and what the teacher wants the child to do are dichotomous.

Throughout this chapter I refer to the Dunce as 'he', because that is the way Prévert writes about him in the poem. In the workshops the Dunce should not be gender specific. You should make that clear before starting on any drama work.

1. Workshops with children in Years 5, 6 and 7

Read the poem aloud, asking the children to try to shut their eyes and imagine what is happening in the poem, to visualise it. Discuss the poem; initially focusing on how they visualise it, allowing for, validating and encouraging different responses. Make sure that no child feels that because their understanding of it is different from others, they have got it wrong. Try to get away from the notion that there is a correct way of reading a poem.

When children feel confident about the diversity of their own responses to the poem, ask if there is anything anyone does not understand. It's at this point that at least one child usually says s/he doesn't understand the words dunce, prodigies and snares.

Enact the poem line by line, making it concrete. This is effectively analysis through action. Depending on the confidence of the children, this could be done individually or in small groups. There is a big difference between this approach, where you are asking children to interpret the poem, actively encouraging diversity of response, and the teacher simply telling the children what to do. In order to enact the poem in this way, interpretative decisions have to made about it. If undertaken seriously, valuing as many contributions as possible, this is a lengthy process. In each case, where a child makes a suggestion, write the suggestion on the board or flip chart, so that you can return to them at a later stage. Where appropriate, ask them to show you what they mean: how, for example, the Dunce might shake his head.

Note the range of diverse responses, some of them contradictory. There is, as yet, no single interpretation of the poem emerging. You are still encouraging children to feel confident in their own responses. It may be that this is as far as you want to take it; that the enactment has itself brought the poem to life, has encouraged the children as active readers and listeners; and, through the discussion that has taken place, encouraged them to think about some of the issues raised by the poem about bullying and resilience.

Literacy skills
Enacting the poem in this way is a process which offers excellent opportunities for developing literacy skills.

Line in poem	Teacher's questions	Examples of responses	Comments
He says no with his head	How does he say no with his head? What does he do?	Looks around, shakes his head. Sits on his chair, slumped.	Even with the first question, encourage responses that pay attention to detail. You might therefore pick up on 'looks around', asking what he sees, using the opportunity to remind everyone that the world of the poem is a fictional world, 'not our classroom, not this school'.
But he says yes with his heart	How does he say 'yes with his heart'?	He wants to answer the teacher's questions, but says no with his head because he fears the other children will mock him for his knowledge. He smiles.	This is a sophisticated response, linking the first two lines of the poem. Many of the individual lines in the poem only make sense when enacted in relation to the broader context; and decisions about one affect others.

Line in poem	Teacher's questions	Examples of responses	Comments
he says yes to what he loves	What does he love? Give examples. You might need to qualify this question (perhaps asking what makes him feel really happy) in order to get beyond a list of favourite foods.	Dinosaurs. Animals. His friends, his sports mates. His dog. His pets. Computer games.	For the teacher, responses to this can be very revealing. The poem opens a dichotomy between the things that the child loves and the things that the teacher wants him to do. This provides a golden opportunity for the teacher at a later stage of the workshop to return to these, the things that the Dunce loves.
he says no to the teacher	*How* does he say 'no to the teacher'? Does he speak? Body language. *Where* is he when he says no to the teacher?	He shakes his head. He doesn't speak. He sticks his tongue out. He is still at his table. It's a table where he has to sit on his own.	The structure of the poem itself encourages a non-literal response, the first line drawing attention to other ways of saying no than speaking the word aloud.

Line in poem	Teacher's questions	Examples of responses	Comments
he stands	How does he stand?	Slowly. Quickly. Shyly. Aggressively.	Note the contradictory responses. It is the teacher's job here to value each of these and to reflect on the possible meanings of each. At this stage you do not have to agree on one; better to talk about the different ways that people show feelings
he is questioned	Who asks the question(s)?	The teacher. His mum. His Dad. Every adult he has contact with.	Most children say 'the teacher'; but if, as noted, there are other responses, you can explore some of those in depth at a later stage.
	What specific questions are asked?	What were we talking about? What did I just say? Where's your homework? Why didn't you bring your gym kit?	

Line in poem	Teacher's questions	Examples of responses	Comments
and all the problems are posed	What problems?	Problems of being in school, unable to do work that makes him feel bad about himself.	One of the points where it's helpful to discuss the different ways in which people feel lacking in confidence. The teacher could give a lead, perhaps talking about her own feelings of anxiety when at school.
			This might provide an opportunity to talk about the ways that some problems come from inside us and some from outside. The fiction of the poem creates a kind of safety zone, in which children can use the Dunce to talk about themselves more freely than they might otherwise be able to.
Sudden laughter seizes him	What does this mean? Can you show me?	He laughs uncontrollably and loudly. He laughs, but tries to keep it quiet, within himself.	

Line in poem	Teacher's questions	Examples of responses	Comments
and he erases all the words and figures names and dates	What does he do?	He forgets the bullying and the humiliation that happens at school and goes quiet. He tears up the paper he has been working at. He goes to the front of the class and wipes the whiteboard clean.	As elsewhere, try to enact each of the suggestions. This may then need a subsequent question along the lines of 'What do other people see when he forgets …?' Although much of the poem deals with an internal world of anxieties and fears, it is the enactment which enables the richness of the discussions.
sentences and snares	What does this mean? Give examples of questions that are traps – that he cannot answer.	That some of the questions are traps. That he feels the teacher and the other children in school gang up against him, that they want to catch him out. 'What did I just say?' 'What are you thinking about?'	Depending on the experience and ability of the children it might be appropriate to ask why the specific questions are traps. This is dependent upon the abilities and articulacy of the children.

Line in poem	Teacher's questions	Examples of responses	Comments
and despite the teacher's threats	What specifically does the teacher threaten?	Sending him to the headteacher. Getting him to stand outside the classroom. Taking a letter home to his parents.	It may be necessary at this point to remind them again that the dramatised enactment of the poem is set in an imaginary school.
	Why is the particular threat so troubling to him?	Because he's been to the head before, and this time it might mean he'll be suspended. Because his Dad is mean to him.	
to the jeers of infant prodigies	What specifically are the jeers?	They call him names. Throwing bits of scrunched up paper at him.	It might be appropriate to ask here what the teacher does when some of the children call the Dunce names or throw paper at him.
	Why 'infant prodigies'? This could be rephrased in several different ways – such as: 'In the poem, who thinks that some of the other children in the class are prodigies?'	It's only the Dunce who thinks the others are 'prodigies'. Some of the other class think he's the one who's a prodigy.	This response opens up the possibility of discussing difference, and how people view difference. It's particularly important to structure this part of the enactment safely. One way is to

Line in poem	Teacher's questions	Examples of responses	Comments
	Why does the Dunce think that the others are 'prodigies'?	Because they are the teacher's favourites.	ask them to talk through the calling of names before asking for a volunteer, so that person knows what they're letting themselves in for.
with chalk of every colour on the blackboard of misfortune he draws the face of happiness.	What does he do?	He goes to the board and draws a big smiley face. He stands on his chair and draws a smiley face in the air with his finger. He goes to the front of the class and smiles at everyone.	The reflective comments that the teacher offers here will not only have a powerful effect on the quality of the work that follows, but could also give individual children a strong boost to their own confidence.

2. Suggestions for further work

It would be possible to develop the work individually or in small groups; but in order to maximise the opportunities for artistic and social learning you need to develop a more collaborative creative process.

Stress the importance of all the individual contributions made thus far; and talk about how you are now going to make a play together, loosely based on the poem; that this will be a play which will use everyone's ideas.

Go back over the poem, again acting out each line, but this time taking one suggestion at a time and working with that until all feel positive about it. One way of facilitating this is for the teacher to take on a role or roles, and ask the children to direct – a kind of Forum Theatre. That way you can try out different possibilities. Thus, the teacher might play the Dunce sitting slumped on a chair as the enactment of him saying 'no with his head'. This also makes the role safer for children, who might be unwilling to take on the role themselves for fear of the mockery that is at the heart of the poem itself.

Line by line, you build up a collaborative, agreed enactment of the poem.

Depending on how you wish to develop the work from here, this collective enactment can now be performed, used as one scene in a play, or as a starting point in a process drama – see below.

Populating the drama

However you wish to use the enactment, the next stage is to think about who is involved in it. Make a list of all those people not mentioned in the poem itself with whom the Dunce might have contact during a week. Depending on the children's abilities and experience of this kind of work, this task could be undertaken as a whole class, with suggestions noted on the board, individually, or in small groups. Start by thinking about the people directly implied by the poem, the teacher and the 'infant prodigies', and work out from there. The resulting lists have included:

- Mum (sometimes a single Mum)
- Dad (sometimes a single Dad)
- Gran (sometimes acting as a parent)
- brothers and sisters
- neighbours
- shopkeepers
- bus driver

- lollypop lady
- dinner Ladies
- caretaker
- school ancillary staff
- other teachers in the school
- school friends
- educational psychologist
- social worker

Ask for suggestions as to what any of these people might say about the Dunce, encouraging difference. To share this, ask them to step forward, say who they are, and then give their comment. For example:

Dinner lady: He's always in trouble, that one
Shopkeeper: Nice lad. Always smiling

It's important to seek opportunities to reflect on these comments, acknowledging the apparent contradictions, in this instance perhaps saying, 'I wonder why different people see him in such different ways?'

Through these short snippets of dialogue, which can be presented in montage form, you can build up a picture of the Dunce's social world, perhaps creating a sequence of short dialogues representing the range of different ways that people see him. Each of the two line snippets of dialogue can then be developed into slightly longer scenes – in small groups, through Forum Theatre, or through whole class discussion. Throughout this process, it's important to encourage positive thinking about the Dunce, the child who is different, acknowledging that there are times when all of us feel different.

Working with objects. Objects as metaphors.
The poem includes the line 'He says yes to what he loves.'
Go back to the question in the original enactment: 'What does he love?'
In workshops with children, responses to this question have included:

- dinosaurs
- his dog or pets
- wild animals
- swimming in the sea
- texting his friends
- playing football
- playing computer games

These range from topics of interest to actions. The responses are likely to give you an indication of what the children are interested in exploring. I have been surprised by how often responses to the question have suggested that the Dunce is an isolate; and how keen they have been to explore the world of the isolate. Perhaps I should not be surprised given children's anxieties about feeling different, feeling on the edge of their peer group.

Choose a specific object which represents the Dunce's attachment to what he loves – preferably things which class members can bring in to school. With dinosaurs, animals or a pet this might be a picture, a photograph or a book; with the actions, perhaps an item of clothing, a ball, a pair of boots, or a frisbee.

Dramatise a sequence of moments when the object is important – for example when he was given a book as a present.

If the group, or groups, have difficulty with this, you might make the task more specific: make five still images to show a story that develops around the use of the object, a sequence of frozen plot moments. The story is about how a conflict arises and is resolved.

The sequence might, for example, work as follows:

1. Dunce and sibling are doing something ordinary together (having a picnic, waiting in a meal queue, catching a bus) – *not* watching TV if at all possible!
2. There is a minor upset, a misunderstanding or disagreement about the chosen object.
3. The minor upset results in a conflict.
4. Attempts are made to resolve the conflict – possibly involving a third party.
5. Conflict is finally resolved.

Make the images. Share with larger group. Add speech bubbles or dialogue. Group or individuals take the images and use the speech bubble suggestions as they see fit to develop each scene in the sequence.

What is the significance of the object in each of the scenes? What does the object mean to each of the people in the scenes? Why is it more important to one than other(s)? What do the different people's attitudes to the object reveal about them and their situation?

In reflecting on the five scenes, it is worth drawing attention to the dramatic structure of this short sequence – which is in classical form. The short sequence of scenes with dialogue is in effect a five act play, albeit a short one.

Suggestions for process drama

In order to develop this material as a process drama, you need a more collective approach, although creating an interpretation of the poem through collaborative enactment could provide a powerful starting point.

Detailed accounts of projects of process drama are provided in *The Kraken*, *The Arrival* and *The Fall of Troy*, so the following suggestion is offered as a brief indication of how the material could be used in this way. The central question, 'Who are we and what is the problem we are trying to solve?' is essentially the same as in playwriting. The difference is that within a process drama the fictional world offers a context which embraces, supports and protects the participants; and the participants act as an audience to their own work, alternating between enactment and reflection.

> The enacted poem is treated as if it were a video document, as evidence in an investigation into the behaviour of the Dunce prior to his exclusion from school. The class then take on the role as experts, questioning different people involved, and ultimately working with the Dunce, the parents, the teachers and the Dunce's classmates to get him reinstated.

3. Workshops with student teachers

I have also used *The Dunce* in workshops with student teachers. With these groups, work on the poem provided a way of encouraging the participants to see bad behaviour in school as a problem to be addressed rather than as a manifestation of malevolence; a way of directly addressing the fears that many young teachers have of confrontation and not being able to keep control. The Forum style approach enabled them to try out strategies in a safe environment in exactly the way that children can in drama, it enabled them to play at bad behaviour, to laugh at themselves, and to escape the notion of the problem child as an adversarial other.

The sessions were driven by key organising questions such as:

- how might we deal with a gifted child who is disruptive?
- how might we deal with children who intimidate each other?

■ how can we seek assistance when we encounter disruptive children without becoming demoralised?

■ how might we allow a child who sees herself as an outsider develop a voice?

The starting point was to create a sequence of still images of the events in the poem from the point of view of:

■ Dunce
■ class teacher
■ parent of another child
■ parent of the Dunce
■ headteacher
■ other children in the class
■ an Ofsted Inspector

Discussions

■ their own experiences of (and possibly as) children labelled as a Dunce

■ what do they think happens in the poem?

■ how do they read the Dunce's behaviour?

■ why do they think he behaves as he does?

■ identify your own contradictory responses to the Dunce and show these in a montage of still images, which others can then discuss and to which thoughts, feelings, hopes, fears and anxieties can then be added in spoken or written form

■ how to create an appropriate learning environment for such a child?

Writing in role

The events of the poem from the point of view of the Dunce. How does he remember that day? If it's decided that the child cannot write, the exercise could take the form of a transcript of what the Dunce says to a parent when he gets home.

This is a useful exercise for student teachers, demanding that they see behavioural problems from the point of view of the problem.

Thoughts, fears, anxieties, dreams – of the Dunce, Dunce's parent(s), the teacher, a student teacher working in the class. Still images, short improvisations.

125

Exploring the social context. Examining the way that the relationships be-tween the children in the class interlace with the wider social environment. Might start with similar exercises to that described above with different people talking about the Dunce.

Forum Theatre

How to persuade or encourage:

- Headteacher to spend money on appropriate classroom assistance for a child such as the Dunce
- class teacher not to dismiss the Dunce
- other children in the class to stop bullying the Dunce
- a reluctant, timid, child to participate in classroom activities

In each case it is important to ensure that the level of difficulty is appropriate to the group, that the Forum is structured so that they can achieve success.

Years 6 and above
The Arrival
by Shaun Tan

Planning a process drama
Metaphor and symbol
Shifting points of view
Emotional maps
From process drama into performance
Writing and reading role
Descriptive writing
Observation

The Arrival by Shaun Tan is a graphic novel about migrants' experiences of leaving the Old Country, travelling across the sea, then arriving and settling in a New World. In Shaun Tan's words, *The Arrival* is

> a wordless story that draws on the conventions of silent cinema and surrealism, a migrant story told as a series of wordless images. A man leaves his wife and child in an impoverished town, seeking better prospects in an unknown country on the other side of a vast ocean... With nothing more than a suitcase and a handful of currency, the immigrant must find a place to live, food to eat and some kind of gainful employment. He is helped along the way by sympathetic strangers, each carrying their own unspoken history: stories of struggle and survival in a world of incomprehensible violence, upheaval and hope. (Tan, 2006 http://www.shauntan. net/books/the-arrival.html) (June 2008)

Several illustrations from the book are reproduced on this website.

About the book

The book is presented as if it were a battered old photograph album – with creases and stains printed onto the pages and the illustrations presented and organised on the pages as if they were old photographs.

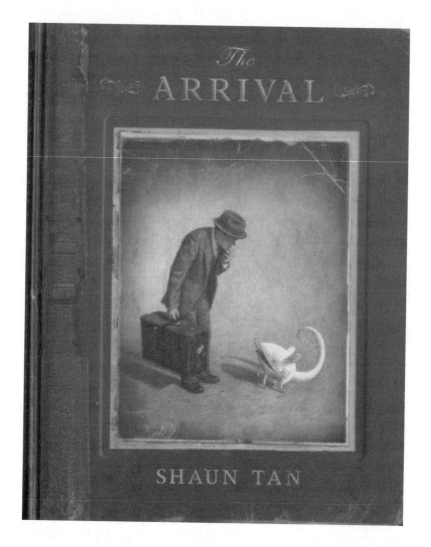

In the opening pages of the book, the images look familiar, as if they might have originated in a Polish ghetto in the late 1930s. Gradually, however, as the world of the central character becomes unstable, the threats to him, his family and their way of life are presented in such a way as to make the images less historically specific. He and numerous others emigrate. In spite of appalling conditions at sea, they carry with them powerful and positive memories of those they have left behind and great hopes for the future. When the migrants arrive in the New World, they find it strange and deeply confusing. It reminds us of New York, but the images are surrealistic, unsettling. It's a world in which nothing is quite as familiar as it at first seems – either to the immigrants or to a reader. The immigrants are strangers in a strange land.

Using *The Arrival* for drama

There are numerous ways in which the book might be used to initiate drama. The graphic novel format, which sometimes resembles the storyboard for a film, creates an open text which is powerfully resonant with known histories, and yet evocative of otherness. Its power arises through the quality of the imagery and Tan's ability to combine the familiar with the unfamiliar. One of the many achievements of Tan's book is to stimulate the imagination without tying it down.

Although the material presented here works best when used with a copy of *The Arrival*, it does not demand a knowledge of the book by either the teacher or the children.

The following material is organised into six sections:

1) **Plan for a process drama using *The Arrival* as a starting point**

2) **Possibilities for a process drama. An indication of how a process drama might develop out of these planning suggestions**

3) **Suggestions for literacy and writing in role activities**

4) **Using the methodology of process drama to develop material towards performance**

5) ***The Arrival* as a stimulus for playwriting activities**

6) **Further resources**

Format

In Part 2, text on the left of the page offers suggestions for work; text on the right contains comment and analysis.

1 Planning for a process drama

In the early stages of planning, try to consider the following:

- Who might be involved in the drama – possible roles for participants, possible roles for teacher/leader?

- What **problem**(s) might the participants be trying to solve?

- What are the **key questions** around which to organise the drama? What will be the focus of the drama?

■ What dramatic **frame**(s) might be used in order to explore this material safely?

■ How are we going to develop the fictional world of the drama, and how are we going to develop the commitment of the participants in the drama to this fictional world, in order that they can explore the material in safety and in depth?

■ How can the teacher present the material to the participants in a way which engages their attention quickly?

The planning process should be flexible. It is, for example, sometimes better to start with a **key question**, and then think about the roles that people might take.

The notes below are an indication of a range of *possibilities*; responses to the above. They are not intended to be in any way prescriptive.

In practice it is best not make a final decision about the actual key questions, focus and frame until after you have met the group and have assessed what the participants are likely to find most engaging, stimulating, challenging and rewarding.

Who (some possibilities – there are many others)

■ emigrants

■ immigrants

■ oppressors in the Old Country

■ friends and neighbours left behind in the Old Country

■ emigration Officers

■ ship's crew

■ ship owners

■ officers who make decisions

■ deck hands and seamen who deal directly with migrants

■ immigration Officers

■ new neighbours in the New World

■ potential and actual employers in the New World

■ second/third generation settlers looking back at, or researching, the experiences of their ancestors

What problems might the participants be trying to solve?

Emigrants

- can we find make a new life in another country?
- what to leave behind?
- what to take with you?
- how to hold on to the memories of those you have left behind?
- after arriving in the New World – how do you balance the need to make a new life with the need to hold on to what you value of the old?

Ship's crew

- where are we to put these people when the ship is already over-loaded?
- how do you deal with the competing pressures – to carry out orders and to remain humane in your dealings with these people?

Immigration Officers

- how can we keep this country safe and healthy for those who have already made their homes here at great personal sacrifice?
- who do we allow to enter the country?
- what criteria do we adopt for making decisions?
- how can we be fair if those in authority over us are trying to force us to make decisions we believe to be morally wrong?

New neighbours in the New World

- how can we find out about these new arrivals in our country when they don't speak our language or understand our customs, our way of life?
- how do we deal with the threats these new arrivals seem to pose to our way of life?

Key questions

The question(s) should be something that you hold in your head as you work through the process, using it to guide decision making. At some point in the dramatic process you may want to share it with the group, but not necessarily at the beginning. This will depend on the group, and also on the nature of the question. It may be helpful to share it at the beginning; but it may be too intimidating to the group.

The concept of the key question is helpful both at the planning stage and during the dramatic process itself. It allows you flexibility whilst giving the work a strong sense of purpose and direction. The questions should not be something which can be easily answered! It may be that there can never be simple, single answers to such questions.

It is likely that it will relate to one or more of the problems noted above.

Some examples that arise directly out of the material above:

- how do people balance the need to make a new life with the need to hold on to what they value of the old?
- how can we relate to people when they seem not to understand our customs, our way of life or our language?
- how do we support people who appear to refuse our help?
- how can people hold on to their own identity when the certainties in their world have disappeared?
- how do we deal with orders from those who employ us, when we feel that those orders are morally wrong; and yet disobeying those orders is likely to result in hardship for those whom we love?

Frame

The following discussion of the concept of the Dramatic Frame is adapted and developed from my book, *The Teaching of Drama in the Primary School*:

When planning and organising a process drama you are essentially thinking about a sequencing of activities and episodes. As you're doing this you should also consider the point of view from which those episodes are seen.

In 'real life', we see the world through our own eyes. Events unfold as they happen. Moments which we would like to savour disappear in a flash and moments which embarrass us seem interminable. Drama enables us to slow down time, to focus on moments which would otherwise pass by without notice, to attend to detail; it enables us to juxtapose events which in 'real life' might be separated by time and space, to seek out patterns. Drama allows us to make the familiar strange, allows us a glimpse of new possibilities – in ourselves and in others.

It is this manipulation of time and viewpoint which enables us to choose an appropriate frame through which to explore our dramatic situations. Thus you can examine any given sequence of events dramatically by seeing these events through different eyes, or you can look at the same events from a distance by framing your drama as an investigation or an enquiry. (Woolland, 1993)

Possible frames for _The Arrival_:

Real time – chronology moving forwards

Participants as emigrants deciding to leave. Pressures. Repression. Why leave home? What to leave? What to take? On board the ship. Arriving in the New World. Memories.

External Investigations

Participants as investigators looking for illegal immigrants and seeking out their stories. Teacher might well take on the role of an immigrant. The drama in this instance might start by developing the roles of the investigators, so that they develop an awareness of the pressures on them to deliver results. It would then gradually reveal the moral complexities of this position.

Internal investigations

Participants as second generation settlers, looking back at their own histories. Who are we, how did we get here? Who do you talk to in order to find out what you want to know? How do you talk to people to find out?

In this frame, the images from _The Arrival_ might take on the status of evidence. The drama might start by TiR showing group the image of the people huddled on deck, saying, 'My grandfather used to work on ships before WW2. This was something I found in the attic, along with a set of documents.'

2 Possibilities for a process drama

Principles of working

It's important early on to establish the principles of _collective_ creativity, of bringing the specific fictional environment to life in a way which asks for each contributor to honour and build on other contributions. Thus, if the group are in role as immigrants on the deck of the boat, and one person says, 'All I can see is the rain and the heavy grey clouds,' all have to accept that is the way the weather is. If one person then says, 'I can see sunshine', try to _incorporate_ that into the developing fiction, to work collectively to read that contribution in a way which allows it to complement the earlier observation about the rain.

It is likely that some members of any class will have first hand experience of being immigrants and most classes in urban schools will include children whose parents are second or third generation immigrants. There will be many opportunities in this drama to discuss the class members' own experiences, which it is important to recognise and respect. I have noted some, though not all of these opportunities below. The drama offers the protection of fictionalisation.

The following is not a scheme of work, but rather an indication of some possible episodes in an evolving, extended process drama. In practice, any drama based on this material should diverge from this model, which is not an account of a sequence of workshops or classes with one group, but a collation of workshops undertaken with several different groups.

The project assumes that the group has seen the first part of *The Arrival*, that they are familiar with some of the images; and that the teacher has undertaken preparatory work discussing possible reasons for people choosing to leave a way of life and endure considerable hardships in the hope of finding a new life in a New World.

The *key questions* informing this drama are:

■ How can people hold on to their own identity when the certainties in their world have disappeared?

■ How do we deal with orders from those who employ us, when we feel that those orders are morally wrong; and yet disobeying those orders is likely to result in hardship for those whom we love?

The drama
Twilighting

Using the picture of emigrants on deck as a stimulus, whole group create a still image which represents this image.

Teacher asks one child, 'If you look out beyond the deck of the boat, what do you see?'

Note the question, 'What do you *see*?' rather than 'What do you *feel*?'

Focusing on the visual, allows the teacher to push the responses towards greater specificity. Later, when the sense of place has become concrete, questions about feelings are likely to be more valuable because they go beyond the generalised.

Responses might include: 'I see ... rain... clouds ... a storm coming this way... skyscrapers...'

Teacher values these responses, encouraging involvement in the roles by *wondering* about the responses of the people who see these things – 'I wonder how people cope when conditions are so bad...'

Develop the visual: 'And what do you see on the ship? On the deck?'

'Who else do you know here on deck?'

The children thus create roles for each other: 'He used to be the baker in the town we came from,' 'I saw her when she came into my shop...'

> If the social health of the group is poor, it may be that the teacher will need to be more interventionist. An alternative approach would be to discuss the roles before the children choose their own; but most groups respond very positively to this method of creating roles for each other, finding it pleasurable in itself. The allocation of roles becomes part of the developing drama, rather than an administrative task.

Teacher in role
Teacher takes on a role as a member of the ship's crew.

'I'd like to help you people, but there is no space below decks. We warned you that the ship was full. We warned you what it would be like. We warned you about storms. Well, there's a big one coming. You need to prepare yourselves. I'll help you as best I can, but I've got my own work to be getting on with.'

> The actual words could well draw on some of the things that the children have themselves said in response to the opening question, 'What do you see?'

When everybody is ready for the storm, the *teacher as narrator* reflects on the group's decisions and actions, drawing significance from the work and taking the drama forwards. 'These people had already made such sacrifices in leaving their old lives behind, their way of life, their friends, many of their belongings... I wonder what each of them was thinking about as they huddled, trying to protect themselves and each other from the storm?'

Teacher spotlights some of the children, asking what they remember of their old way of life.

The storm is enacted by means of a technique which Brecht used in rehearsals: the teacher asks the children one by one to narrate in the third person whatever each does, thinks and feels. In this instance, one of the children might say, 'The baker is feeling sea sick, but he gets up and goes to help the farmer who has fallen and hurt his leg.' Another might say, 'This man is so frightened by the movement of the ship that he wraps his coat around himself and shuts his eyes. He wonders if any of them will survive this journey.'

> It can help to discuss possible reactions first, without pre-planning them, and start the enactment from an agreed still image. There are several advantages of this technique:

- It slows the action down at moments like this, which could otherwise become unfocused

- It can draw attention to the difference between what people think, feel and do

- It creates a safety net around the depiction of violence and high emotion.

Discussions

- What were you able to take with you, and what do you still have with you now?

- What is the thing that is most precious?

- Who did you have to leave behind?

- What do you hope for in the New World?

- What specifically do you imagine life will be like?

  The following discussion might usefully be informed by looking at relevant research materials – see below – or at more of the pictures in *The Arrival*.

These discussions inform the subsequent *writing in role* activities. When the storm is over, the teacher asks the group to write letters to those left behind in the Old World, to tell them about the voyage, whilst trying to assure them that you're safe.

The letter writing could take several other forms: diary entries, lists of what you have with you, what you left behind. The writing thus becomes not only a means of reflecting on the condition of the emigrants, but also of developing a deeper engagement with the roles.

Here, it may be useful to refer to pictures in *The Arrival*, in this instance of the man writing in a notebook, and then tearing out the page and making it into a paper bird.

Teacher then narrates again:

'There is one old man here who has not spoken to anybody.' Teacher creates an image of the man on the cover of the book.

The construction of this character could be a collaborative process. The character could even be dressed by the children from various clothes which the teacher has brought in, the children selecting those they think appropriate. I would recommend, however, that you find and bring in the suitcase and do not tell the children what you have decided to put in it. This then creates a powerful image and a narrative enigma.

When the children are satisfied with the image, the characterisation, that they have created, the teacher moves briefly out of role and narrates again:

'I wonder why this old man is so alone? I wonder what the other people on the deck say about him? I wonder what rumours there are?'

This could again provide opportunities for written work – perhaps leading to a short playwriting exercise: noting down in dialogue form the exchanges that have taken place between the emigrants and the old man.

> Creating this picture of the old man alone with his enigmatic case is a good place to end this particular episode of the drama. It creates a powerful image to which you can return, which the immigrants will each remember in their own way; and which leaves questions hanging in the air – who is the old man, what will happen to him, and what is in his case?
>
> It would be possible to continue with the drama, following the chronology of *The Arrival*. For this example, however, I wish to demonstrate how learning opportunities in the drama can arise from shifting points of view. One of the benefits of working on a process drama over several weeks is that it enables you to explore material from different points of view – particularly useful with this material. The next session might take place a week or more later. The work that has been done developing engagement with and commitment to the roles of the immigrants is, however, necessary in order for the subsequent work to be productively challenging.

The teacher explains that we are now going to move forward to a point some time after the immigrants have arrived in the New World. The aim will be to create small family groups, through pair work and small group improvisation. First it may be useful to look carefully at some of the pictures in *The Arrival* (for example of the newspaper boy with the incomprehensible advertising banner), and to talk about the kind of feelings that they evoke, about feelings of difference, of being an outsider.

Writing in role
Written responses in role to images from *The Arrival*.

These could take various forms:

- journal entries
- a letter to an immigrant friend you haven't seen since entering the country
- a letter to a relative in the Old World, trying to convince that person that you are having a wonderful time, that the hardships of the journey were all worth it; or warning them not to follow

In each family group there are two adults (siblings, cousins, not necessarily man and wife) and two dependants – an older person and child. The purpose of the improvisations will be to create the sense that the family is more impoverished in the New World than they were in the Old, and that any decision about work made by the adults affects the two dependants.

Short improvisations

- adult going for interviews and being turned down for work

- adult looking for work, asking strangers where there might be work

- adult couple arguing about why they have not been able to get work

- old person telling grandchild stories about the voyage from the Old World to the New

Experienced, able children could undertake this task as pair group improvisations with a short time limit. They could alternatively could be enacted using the techniques of Forum Theatre with the teacher taking on one of the roles, or developed from a series of still images.

Small group improvisations

A family meal intended as a celebration, but with very little food to go round. What are they celebrating?

> The method of dramatising this will depend on the ability and experience of the children – from structured still images, through Forum Theatre to free improvisation with a time constraint.

After the enactment of the meal, however, it is important to make time to reflect on it:

'What do we learn about these people from this scene, about how they are coping with the disappointment that the New World is not as they expected it?'

At the Port Authority

Teacher narrates:

'After several weeks, the family were getting desperate. There seemed no hope of work. They had used all the savings they had; and then one of them found a notice in the street with a map on it; and took it home. It was an advertisement for workers at the Port Authority.'

Document creation

Making the advertisement for workers. Small group task.

Forum Theatre

Teacher interviews a volunteer member of the class – who represents all those who are seeking work, for a job at the Port Authority. 'The work will be difficult and you will have to work very long hours.' During the interview there is no mention that it will entail screening new immigrants as they enter the country.

Discussion

- ■ What will people working for the Port Authority be required to do?
- ■ Which immigrants will be allowed in, which will be turned away? What criteria will be used to make these decisions?

With guidance, some able and experienced children might be able to tackle these problems in small groups. For others, it would be better undertaken as a whole group discussion. In either case, the tasks would be more meaningful supported by some preliminary research work.

Creation of further documents. These could draw on pictures from *The Arrival*, and might include:

- questionnaires for immigrants to complete
- identity tags
- travel documents

In pairs, everyone is asked to practice the work they will have to do at the Port Authority; one playing the interviewer, the other playing an immigrant.

Formalised enaction
What might the worker's thoughts be as s/he gets his/her first wage packet?

Discussion of possible range of responses, followed by

Writing in role
Make a list of the things you plan to spend your wages on.

Returning home with your first wage, and trying to avoid telling the rest of the family where you are working and what you have to do.

The old man and the suitcase
Teacher narrates:

'One day, when X had begun to get used to the work at the Port Authority, s/he found him/her self having to deal with an old man who had been waiting several weeks at the port. When his ship had arrived, everybody else on it had passed quickly through immigration control. But because he had no relatives waiting for him, because he could not speak the language, because none of the other immigrants on the ship seemed to know him, he had to wait.'

Volunteer, now acting as the person working for the Port Authority, has to interview the old man, with the teacher taking on the role of the old man.

Preparatory discussion, likely to include:

- What do you need to try to find out from him?
- How will you try to communicate with him if he doesn't speak our language?

141

■ reminders that the worker's family needs the wage s/he is bringing home from this job, that allowing someone to enter the country without proper documentation could result in getting sacked.

It's important to slow this exchange down, to make visible the pressures and tensions that are acting on the port authority worker. The principle is the same as that underpinning the enactment of the storm. You need to find a technique which will simultaneously protect the class and keep them engaged in the deep dilemmas of the situation. There is no single right way of doing this. The following suggestion offers one possible way of achieving it.

Teacher plays the old man. A volunteer from the class stands beside the old man and speaks his thoughts/feelings. A class member plays the port authority worker. A volunteer stands beside her/him and voices thoughts/feelings.

The interview is conducted as Forum Theatre – with the volunteers able to stop the enactment and ask advice from the audience, or ask someone else to take over their role. At any stage the teacher can step out of role and guide the class.

The use of Forum Theatre at this point, with formalised thoughts and feelings added, is partially to ensure the engagement of the whole class in the situation and partially to protect the child who plays the Port Authority worker.

The teacher, as the old man clinging to the suitcase, makes this as difficult as the class can manage, speaking in a language none of them can understand or in a form of gibberish, making it difficult for the port worker to be sympathetic, difficult to allow the old man entry into the country.

At some point in the interview, the old man could open the suitcase – potentially a moment of high dramatic tension. The class will probably have wanted to know about what it contains from their first sight of it. What you place in it is up to you. You might discuss out of role with the class what they would like the contents to be – a very empowering strategy through which they can learn much about dramatic structure. When I have worked on this material with children and students I have used ideas from *The Arrival*. My suitcase has contained some old clothes, a child's drawing based on the one in the middle of the first page of Section I of *The Arrival*, a picture frame with family portrait – the first image of Section II – and a chipped teapot.

Discussion out of role about these objects. Why has he carried these things with him? Why might he think them so important?

From here on the drama becomes more open. If they decide to grant the old man entry to the country, you might follow the possible consequences – the worker having to argue for his/her job; how is the old man going to look after himself in this hostile environment? To conclude this chapter I assume that the worker refuses him entry.

Writing in role

The port worker's report. How does s/he write about the interview to the boss? What is the recommendation?

Teacher in role, as a senior officer at the Port Authority, announces that all those who have been refused entry will have to stay in quarantine for two weeks until a ship is ready to take them back where they came from.

> Here, the teacher addresses the whole class, who function as a Greek Chorus. Their responses are simultaneously individual and collective.

> The two weeks is important because it gives time within the fiction for the class to organise a collective response to the denial of entry.

Discussion out of role: how will the worker talk about the interview to the rest of the family? How might the family respond?

Small group improvisations

Family meal: a reprise of the earlier meal, but this time although the family has enough money to provide food, the worker has to deal with the memories of turning away the old man.

Diary entries

What does each person think and feel about the news that the old man has been turned away?

Teacher: 'In real life we wouldn't be able to see the old man. In real life we certainly couldn't talk to him. His language is different. But in drama we can find out more about him. I wonder what he's going through at this point? I wonder what he has to return to in the Old Country? It has been very hard for these families, they have struggled with no work, no money and very little food, but in spite of occasional arguments they have had each other for support. He has been alone through everything.' (The exact words will reflect the situations that the class has developed through the drama).

Teacher takes on role as the old man again.

Small groups prepare to talk to him. What do you want to ask him? What do you want to say to him? Each group to prepare no more than three questions and three statements.

> Limiting the number of questions encourages the groups to give careful thought to the questions they will ask. They will need further guidance to ensure they don't waste questions. The class are not taking on specific roles here, they are again functioning as a kind of Chorus. Their questions and statements will allow the man's hidden story to become visible. What this story is will depend on the needs, interests and experiences of the class. It should reveal the reasons for his isolation and evoke sympathy whilst avoiding sentimentality.

Reconciliation

> The reconciliation that needs to occur here is as much with themselves as with the old man. They have all been party to the denial of entry. By having the class themselves play the Port Authority immigration official who turn down the old man's request for entry, you avoid the danger of demonising a faceless bureaucracy, but instead ask questions about the ways in which we inadvertently become complicit with or even part of such a bureaucracy.

Writing in role

Class to create documents intended to persuade the authorities to change their mind and allow the old man to stay. What might these documents be?

A collectively written letter or speech, using these documents as evidence, appealing against the decision to refuse the old man entry into the New World. What arguments should be used? What evidence needed, vocabulary to be used, tone to be adopted in speech or letter? The task could be undertaken as a whole class or in small groups. The delivery of the letter or speech should be made highly significant and formalised. The following is just *one* way of doing this amongst many:

- during preparatory discussion, lists of arguments, documents, vocabulary noted on whiteboard

- class work in small groups, initially deciding on the order in which they wish to make the arguments in their speech

- class discussion of the order of the argument and decisions about documents to be used

- small groups allocated a responsibility, some for producing required documents, others for a section of the speech

- Forum Theatre. Teacher as senior official at the Port Authority. Class member(s) has to read the letter or the speech, appealing against the Port Authority decision. Can call on the rest of the class for advice, ask for someone else to take over

- official gives verdict, explaining reasoning

By taking on this role, the teacher creates opportunities to value the contributions of individuals and reflect on the significance of the class's achievements.

Museum of immigration

In the planning section of this chapter I discussed alternative frames. One possibility, which would enable much of the above to be used in an adapted form, would be to ask the children to take on roles as custodians of a Museum of Immigration, deciding on the kinds of exhibits, which could include video and audio diaries as well as written documentation, reconstructions of particular moments, celebrations of difference between various immigrant groups.

3 Literacy and writing in role activities
In the Old Country

- census return listing those living in a particular street – including details of employment and families

- lists of items to pack when leaving home

- lists of items to be left behind

- letter to be left behind for a friend/relative who is unable/unwilling to travel

- child(ren)'s drawing(s) taken by emigrant in suitcase

- drawing(s) of house and street

- embarkation ticket

- emigration documents

- diary entry including dreams and hopes of the new life with worst fears

- snippets of overheard conversations as emigrants queue to board ship

On board ship
Ship's crew

- instructions for dealing with migrants

- list of items each migrant is allowed to take on board

- telegraphic message received by ship's navigation officer giving warning of bad weather ahead

- ship's log

- diagrams showing where immigrants are to be housed during voyage

Migrants

- snippets of overheard conversations amongst migrants on deck

- notes passed between migrants – searching for friends/relatives they thought were on board, but have not yet seen

- messages in code between migrants – to avoid content being discovered by ship's crew

- letters written from immigrants to families and friends in the Old Country

- diary/journal entry to include: description of conditions on board ship; memories of the Old Country positive and negative

- description of first sight of the New World

At the Port of Entry into the New World
Immigration officers

- questions to be asked by immigration officers at Port of Entry

- memoranda to new immigration officers about strict need to follow rules

- tests that have to be taken by immigrants

- lists of immigrants expected

- records and reports of interview(s) with immigrant(s)

Immigrants

- visas, passports, travel documentation

- conversations between immigrants recorded by Port Authority observers

- petition organised by a group of immigrants, requesting that the authorities change their mind about the forced repatriation of one (or more) of their number

In the New World
Immediately after arriving

- newspaper headlines and articles about the arrival of the ship with immigrants on it (including different perspectives – humanitarian, restrictive, indignant)

- newspaper articles, advertisements, posters – all written in a language (and possibly lettering) not understood by immigrants

- classified advertisements written by immigrants to put in newspaper/shop window seeking accommodation

- directions given to new immigrant by a fellow countryman already settled in New World – how to find a place to live, work, food handouts

- items for use in the New World that might cause confusion because of language difficulties: maps, money, instructions for use of machinery or household gadgets, conditions of employment

- accounts of stories told and stories shared with other immigrants

- census returns – who lives in this block? What employment do they have?

- letters home, trying to assure those left behind that everything is going well; persuading a friend/relative to join them; or warning them not to

- shopping list and menu for celebratory meal

Many years later

- letter to grandchild reminiscing about the experience of immigration

- descriptions of exhibits in a Museum of Immigration.

4 Developing the material towards performance
Reflection
Teacher asks: 'What moments/incidents do *you* remember from the drama?'

Thinking about one of the characters in the drama – an immigrant who ends up working for the Port Authority, the old man, one of the ship's crew – what are the key moments they might remember of these events? Children – individually or in small groups – make pictures of these moments, adding captions, summative dialogue in comic book style.

Collaboratively, create a timeline of all the events which have taken place during the drama; and perhaps of those which have been implied, but not necessarily dramatised, such as the circumstances which have forced the emigrants to leave their homes.

As a whole class, place the pictures they have created on the overall time line or, in small groups, organise the pictures as a storyboard. The storyboard could represent the whole drama, or one character's story.

If the teacher has taken digital photographs during the Drama, these could also be placed on a timeline to indicate where they fit in the overall chronology.

Writing in role – the story the immigrants would like to tell others about their experiences, the story they would like to leave for their own grandchildren to read.

Depending on the scale of the performance you are developing, you might then work in several ways: small groups could each create a short play, comprised of (say) five scenes, chosen from the timeline or storyboard; if you were working on a single play to be performed by the whole class, you might decide on the five scenes and then assign each of the scenes to a different group, who then work on their own section of the overall play.

The performance itself might be part of the fiction of the initial process drama, taking one of the following forms, for example:

- a group of second generation immigrants gathering to create a play about their parents' experiences

- exhibits, videos or museum drama performances in the Museum of Immigration

5 *The Arrival* as a stimulus for playwriting activities

Playwriting activities that could be undertaken independently of a process drama

- cut out a selection of the individual pictures and ask the children to select five of them, and put them into a sequence to create their own storyboard.

- using any one of the one-page storyboards that appear in the book, add captions to each picture and then, where appropriate, dialogue.

Decide who might be just outside the frame – for example in the following page, a doctor, an immigration officer, a police officer, other immigrants in a waiting room; then create still images using these pictures. Add thoughts and feelings to the pictures.

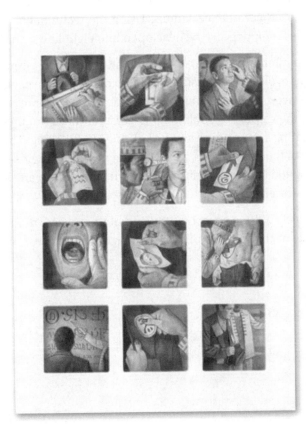

During or after working on *The Arrival* as a process drama

Many of the writing in role activities suggested above could be developed into short scripted scenes. These could become part of the fiction of the process drama. A group of children might work in pairs conducting interviews in the Port Authority Immigration Building, one in each pair group as an immigrant, one as an immigration officer. These interviews, or interrogations, might be recorded and then transcribed. At a later stage in the drama another group might read the transcripts of these interviews with a view to assessing the fairness of the interview technique, or improving refugee resettlement procedures.

At various points in the process drama the teacher is likely to have asked the children to work as a kind of Chorus, for example the moment when the whole group is on the deck of the ship and each child is asked in turn, 'What do you see?' If these comments are recorded, they can themselves be used as snippets of overheard conversations. Using the technique of camouflaging dialogue, these snippets can be developed into eight line scenes.

Once the children are familiar with the material, and an overarching group narrative has evolved, it is possible for them to develop the personal stories of various characters from the drama, for example, those whom we have met on the deck of the ship. They could tell the personal stories of these characters, initially creating a five picture storyboard, one of which might be the image in *The Arrival* of the migrants on deck. To each picture in their storyboard they then have to add two lines of dialogue, which in their turn are developed into six to ten line scenes.

The collectively written speech at the end of the process drama is in itself a fine example of children working as playwrights.

Further Resources

Shaun Tan's website:
http://www.shauntan.net/

The Arrival website
http://www.shauntan.net/books/the-arrival.html

Comments about *The Arrival*:
http://www.shauntan.net/books/the-arrival.html#arrival_comments

Maggie Hulson's *Schemes for Classroom Drama* contains a scheme of work entitled *Refuge*. That specifically examines 'an increasingly complex sequence of dilemmas arising from an internal conflict in an imaginary country.' (Hulson, 2006:42) Although the scheme is devised for Year 8 students, it contains ideas and resources that could be adapted to complement this work on *The Arrival*.

The Museum of London offers various online resources, including *London's Black History*, which could complement and enrich the work.
http://www.museumoflondon.org.uk

The Arrival makes no specific references to the Holocaust, nor to Ellis Island, the location in New York where immigrants were processed on arrival in the USA. Some teachers might, however, find the following Ellis Island web resources useful:
http://teacher.scholastic.com/activities/immigration/tour/index.htm

Photographs of the Warsaw Ghetto can be found on many websites, including: http://www.thornb2b.co.uk/Poland_at_War/Warsaw_Ghetto/Ghetto.htm

'The word *Shoah* is the Hebrew word for gale or violent storm, indicating the turbulent and angry waters of death and pain and grief, that did indeed reach every shore. ... The Shoah Education Project is an attempt to change hearts, to change perspectives, to make us all far more than tolerant of each other.' The authors of the programme claim that it is 'adaptable for all uses.' *The Shoah Education Project* website can be found at:
http://www.shoaheducation.com/

A Teacher's Guide to the Holocaust. This site has substantial teaching and resource materials, including numerous photographs of the Warsaw Ghetto.
http://fcit.usf.edu/holocaust/resource/resource.htm

Year 6 and above
The Fall of Troy

Writing and reading in role
Objects, metaphors, symbols
Dialogue and voice
Dramatic structure
Character
Performance

The material in this chapter assumes that the children have some basic knowledge of stories related to the siege of Troy. Parts 1 and 2 of the drama draw directly on Homer's *The Iliad*, Parts 3 and 4 draw on Virgil's *The Aeneid* and Homer's *Odyssey*. Part 5 briefly indicates how you might develop the work. Part 6 provides an alternative perspective, developing some of the themes around refugees from the previous chapter, *The Arrival*.

The material is intended to complement any work on *Trojan War* stories, focusing mainly on those people who are not mentioned by name in the original, those on the margins of the story; it explores how ordinary people on both sides of the siege might be affected by catastrophic upheaval. The named characters, such as Odysseus, Agamemnon, Achilles, King Priam, Paris and Helen, are seen from the point of view of those whom their decisions affect.

The basic structure of the material below is as follows:

Part 1 The shore outside Troy
Part 2 Inside the walls of Troy
Part 3 Horses and heroes
Part 4 The Wooden Horse
Part 5 Homecoming
Part 6 Guardians of Troy

The first three parts could be used and developed into self-contained schemes of work. Parts 4 and 5 depend on the earlier material and are not self-contained.

The material is devised deliberately to shift points of view in order to open up moral issues. I am not suggesting that you go straight from one part to the next. The shifts of perspective demand careful preparation and discussion.

Each of the first three parts includes material which asks the class to write speeches as part of the drama.

Planning

I have argued elsewhere in this book that one of the simplest prime requisites in planning a drama is to consider who is involved and what problem they are trying to solve. In this project, this changes from one part to another; and can be summarised as follows:

Part	Title	Who	Problems
1	The shore outside Troy	Greek army Odysseus	Do we desert? To persuade the army to stay loyal
2	Inside the walls of Troy	People of Troy	How can we get Hector's body back for a funeral?
3	Horses and heroes	Greek army/ woodworkers Sinon the Greek	How do we end the siege? To persuade the Trojans to take the Wooden Horse into the city
4	The Wooden Horse in Troy	Greeks and Trojans	Not applicable – this part is essentially reflective
5	Homecoming	Greek army	How to come to terms with the destruction we have wrought?
6	Guardians of Troy	Modern day archaeologists	How do we balance the needs of people and the need to protect the cultural heritage of the archaeological site?

It is up to you to decide how open the drama should become. The material is not intended to be prescriptive. The key to using it is in seeing how questions and problems can be used to create learning opportunities.

Preparatory work – twilighting

Sharing knowledge and understanding. What do you know of/remember of the story of Troy, of the Trojan Wars?

Discuss the time in history when the stories are set and how it would have differed from our own. Preparatory work might then include looking at maps of the Aegean Sea, discussion of our modern reliance on machines and gadgets and how people managed without them three thousand years ago.

Small group tasks:
List as many things as possible that you have at home which run on electricity, gas or oil, then:

1. mime a simple activity, using gadgets from today – making breakfast using fridge and gas cooker

2. show how you would achieve the same result by using materials available at the time of the Trojan War – milking the cow, drawing water from the well, chopping firewood, lighting the fire, taking eggs from the chicken...

Part 1 The shore outside Troy

The Greek encampment, memories of the journey, whether to desert
The teacher introduces the drama: 'Our drama is going to start in the Greek camp on the beach outside the walls of Troy.'

Teacher reads aloud the opening lines of Christopher Logue's *War Music*:

> 'Picture the east Aegean sea by night
> And on a shimmering beach, slanting to the sea
> Upwards of fifty thousand men
> Asleep like spoons beside their lethal fleet.
> Now look along that beach, and see....' (Logue, 2001:7)

Teacher asks, 'What do you see?' Using collaborative play making methods outlined on pp134-136, develop a picture of the beach on the Trojan shore.

On a large piece of sugar paper, draw the outline of a dead man on the beach. Add detail – for example, a spear, a sword, a scar on the face.

Teacher in role as a Greek soldier says, 'I am tired of seeing my closest friends die, tired of seeing the bodies of people I have never spoken to, I am tired of waiting here. Our leaders promised us that the siege would last weeks. We have been here nine years. They promised us riches, and I have lost everything. I am tired of war. I know we cannot go home. But I want to honour this man's death. I didn't know him, and I want to honour him.'

The next task of creating a sequence of scenes can thus be contextualised as a way of honouring and remembering the dead man. Ways of doing this might include assembling fragments of the man's life by working with responses to the following questions. Could be done in or out of role.

- Who did he leave behind at home in Greece?
- What was said to him as he left for war?
- What memories or mementoes did he bring with him from home?
- What pictures did he bring with him – of home, of the journey to Troy?
- What memories did he share with anyone – of home, of the journey?
- What were his connections with some of the named Greek characters of *The Iliad* – Achilles, Agamemnon, Patroclus, Calchas the prophet?
- How did he respond to the prophecy that Troy would not fall for *nine years*?
- Did he ever say how he would like to be remembered?
- Does anyone know how he died?

Using these responses, create a chronological time line and/or an emotional map for this man's life. From these create a short sequence of five scenes. This could be done by creating a series of still images, then adding captions and dialogue; or go straight to making the scenes, but with the constraint that each scene is to contain two lines of dialogue.

> At the end of this chapter there is a collection of 25 lines taken from *The Iliad*. Some groups respond positively to the task of having to incorporate one of these lines in each of the scenes.

To deepen the possible meanings, add a prop and/or a simple item of costume to each scene – for example, a garment given by a relative; or, if one of the scenes involves a child, a toy.

Back to the beach. 'We've thought about what you see on the beach, now what do you hear?' Working in small groups, using the musical instruments, voices, create a sound picture of the beach as heard by someone who has woken, but not yet opened their eyes.

Teacher narrates, drawing on the scenes they have created about the dead man, painting a picture of the dreadful conditions, of the conflicts within the army, with many wanting to desert and return home. This not only moves the narrative on, but also creates an opportunity to reflect on the work of the class.

Discussion to prepare for improvisations in pairs, or Forum Theatre:
A has to persuade a colleague to desert; is unwilling to go alone.

B would like to leave the war, feels it is pointless, does not know why they're fighting; but is reluctant to desert.

If A is successful in persuading B, together they secretly make plans, consider how they can find out how many others are going to join them.

Alternatively, a more open improvisation in which both participants are trying to discover how their friend feels about deserting, but both people are frightened that their friend might inform against them.

The preparatory discussion for any of the above should cover:

What has happened to make A decide that now is the time to desert?

Why is B reluctant? Possibly thinks deserting is too dangerous? Possibly for reasons of honour?

After the improvisation or Forum Theatre, summarise the scene in no more than eight lines of dialogue. Stage the scene, making maximum use of body language to indicate caution and secrecy, so that it is hidden from guards, but clear to us, the stage audience.

> If the class are familiar with *The Iliad*, it might be useful at this point to add a narrative summary of the situation in *The Iliad*, where Zeus sends a dream to Agamemnon advising him to plays devil's advocate, encouraging desertion, and deliberately create a situation where Odysseus can step in to give his rabble rousing speech that urges the army on to one final push on Troy.

We reach a *key question* for this part of the drama: *what could Odysseus have said to these exhausted, demoralised people to persuade them to fight, to attack Troy once more?*

Whole group discussion of the kinds of words, the vocabulary that should go into the speech, and then of the kinds of arguments that Odysseus might have used, summarising them under headings – eg patriotism, honour, the promise of Trojan treasures...

We then decide (through whole class discussion or in small groups) on the *order* in which Odysseus might use these arguments in his speech, for example:

1   understanding of the difficulties
2   we have so nearly achieved what we set out for
3   fear of being thought of as cowards
4   patriotism
5   the promise of riches

Thus, collaboratively we start to write the speech that Odysseus might have made to prevent the desertions and urge the army to attack Troy. To enhance the writing we could again use extracts from *The Iliad* as a starting point, incorporating some of these into the speech.

> It is also possible to create a fictional context for this technique of building up a speech using given extracts, placing the speech writing activity itself within the frame of a dramatic fiction. In this instance, the chosen extracts could be written on paper made to look like torn and burnt parchment, and the class might take on the roles of archaeologists who discover these extracts and try to piece them together and fill in the gaps. See Part 6 below.

To complete this part of work we need to find a way of delivering the speeches. We could simply ask one child to volunteer to read the speech aloud to the class, but that risks placing that child at too great a risk, and also ignores the collaborative nature of the process thus far. Instead, we need to formalise the delivery in such a way that the reactions to the speech can be clearly observed and registered. One possibility:

The teacher takes on the role of Odysseus, asking for the help of the class to construct the character, the mode of delivery ('How should I stand? How should I speak? Should I start quietly? ... ') and the setting ('Early morning? Midday? Night? ...') The class stand in a line. Odysseus reads the speech. Moment by moment, each person is to move closer to Odysseus if they feel persuaded to join the final push, to move away if they feel more like deserting.

Part 2 Inside the walls of Troy

Just as *The Iliad* itself switches between the Greeks and the Trojans, so the focus of the drama now moves to the people inside the besieged town of Troy. The aim here is collaboratively to build a sense of Troy, to make it feel 'real' to the participants; to create a sense of a culture with rich traditions.

As preparatory work it would be useful to look at photographs of cultural artefacts from the period, including representations of horses in paintings and statues; and possibly to create a plan of the city.

Teacher in role as a Trojan priest: 'We Trojans are a proud people, renowned throughout the world for our fine city with its lofty gates, fine towers and broad streets. Our defences are strong. The Greeks have been camped outside our walls for nine years and they have not breached the walls of Troy. But now the Greek's hero, Achilles, has slain our noblest warrior, Prince Hector. He has taken the armour from Hector's body and dragged the corpse behind his chariot around the walls of Troy. King Priam, Hector's father, has offered Achilles a ransom of gifts if he will return the body of his son so that we can give him an honourable funeral. Achilles has accepted. I ask you, noble Trojans, each to bring a gift that we can then offer as ransom.'

Making Trojan artefacts – art, design technology task.

Discussion (in or out of role)

What kind of artefacts would make appropriate ransom gifts?

Try to feed in the information that Troy is also renowned for its fine horses; that people of Troy take pride in their expertise as horse tamers and breeders. Artefacts chosen for ransom gifts might include model horses, horse motifs in clothing.

> The artefacts that they make may include drawings of objects; but it would be useful for the teacher to provide some real objects, such as keys that can be handled.

Bringing these artefacts to the priest, laying them down in a formalised, ritualised fashion, describing what they are and the significance they have for each household. The teacher, as priest, sets an example of seriousness, also demonstrating how in the fiction of the drama we can imbue simple everyday objects with weighty significance: showing a chair covered with gold coloured cloth, says 'I will offer this golden throne. It is made of the strongest ebony wood, and covered in gold leaf. The people who crafted it have long since died, but it has been used by the priests of Troy for as long as the city has stood. The survival of the city is more important than one throne. Saving the city is what matters....' Then to the class: 'What gift have you brought; and why is it important?'

> The use of the chair gives a lead – it is simultaneously real with imagined significance – allowing the class to create similar artefacts and for the teacher and the class to work together to endow their artefacts with significance.
>
> The ordinary chair covered in cloth stimulates the imagination. By accepting it as the throne, the class have actively engaged in the fiction, have participated in creating the meaning. If the teacher, as the priest, had offered a model horse sprayed gold, this could well have provoked scepticism – in wanting to know whether it is really gold, they are disengaging from the drama.
>
> The exchange of objects, handling them, begins to make the imagined more concrete, takes us all deeper into the world of the dramatic fiction.

Writing in role
An inventory of artefacts brought to the priest as ransom gifts.

Who will take the gifts to Achilles? What qualities will we seek in someone leaving the safety of the city walls and going to negotiate with Achilles himself?

> Phrasing the question in this way enriches the meaning of the subsequent exchange; it also makes it possible for the teacher to select a child who is usually quiet, whose confidence is likely to be boosted by undertaking the task.

Collaborative writing of the volunteer's speech to Achilles. The method for doing this could follow the same lines as the writing of Odysseus's speech to the Greeks in Part 1.

The encounter between the volunteer and Achilles probably best as Forum Theatre, allowing the volunteer to seek assistance as s/he goes, and for the teacher as Achilles to judge an appropriate level of difficulty in the negotiations. Ultimately, however, Achilles accepts the gifts and allows Hector's corpse to be taken back into Troy.

Teacher narrates: 'The ransom of gifts was taken out of the city walls, and offered to Achilles.' Then uses similar style of narrative voice to reflect on the exchange between Achilles and the Trojan volunteer.

Ritual – the funeral of Hector. Discussion – how do we, the Trojans, make this funeral special?

Enactment of the funeral, followed by reflection. The teacher, out of role, asks for the thoughts and feelings of the Trojans at this time.

To conclude: some possible improvisations. Most of these are for pairs, but could also be undertaken by a small group. Could also work as Forum Theatre with whole class contributing:

- A is feeling demoralised and seeks reassurance from B that they will be alright
- A persuades B they should not flee the city now that Hector is dead
- A persuades B that they have a chance to escape the city, and now is the time to go
- rumours that the Greek ships have left, that they have given up, that the beach is empty

Part 3 Horses and Heroes
Greeks making the horse and preparing the deception

This part focuses on the Wooden Horse. *The Iliad* ends before the sack of Troy but the incident is mentioned in Homer's *Odyssey* and Virgil's *Aeneid*. Most of the modern retellings of the myth include the incident.

In the literature, the Greek deception is successful and leads to the destruction of Troy. In the drama, however, we are not trying to recreate history. It may be that when the class gets to the point in the drama where, as Trojans, they are confronted with the horse, they decide *not* to take it into the city. It's important to allow this decision, and then explore the possible consequences.

Teacher narrates an introduction which situates us back on the shore before Troy. This could draw on previous work done by the class or use an extract from *The Iliad* or a modern retelling to set the scene. If you have used Part 2 and the ransom gifts have been accepted by Achilles, then that should be acknowledged in the narrative introduction.

Mantle of the Expert
Teacher in role as an unnamed leader: 'I am glad to have gathered here those in the Greek army who know most about working with wood. We have decided on a plan. Look at the ransom gifts the Trojans have given us in exchange for Achilles letting them take the corpse of their beloved Hector to give him the funeral they say he deserved. He was indeed a noble warrior. But we are no nearer breaching the walls. Look at the gifts. Horses, horses, horses... We'll build a horse, a giant horse, a horse so big our finest warriors will be able to hide inside it. That's why you, who know about wood, who understand how to build with elegance and strength, have been asked to gather here. When the horse is finished and our warriors are hidden inside,

then the rest of the army, those not hidden inside the horse, will take to the ships and we will sail round the coast and wait out of sight until we see the first signs of smoke rising from the city.'

Discussion

- how do the people feel about making the horse, about the plan?
- is there anything to be lost by making the horse?
- how do these wood workers feel about making such a fine artefact when it is to be used as a weapon of war?

Image theatre – a range of attitudes. What is to be gained/lost by making the horse?

Discussions in and out of role

- what skills will be required to make the horse?
- what tools will we need?
- what kind of wood should we use?
- where will we get it from?
- how can we build it out of sight of the Trojans?

Small groups with specific responsibilities, for example, sourcing the wood, bringing the wood to the construction site, designing specific parts of the horse.

Making the horse. In practice this is likely to be a design task, involving art work, drawings – maybe to scale – and possibly small models.

Writing in role

- inventory of what will be required for the making of it
- description of the horse

Playwriting task

Having built the giant horse and hidden our warriors inside it, how will we persuade the Trojans to take it into the city? It may be that the class respond to this question in a novel way, in which case that is where the drama should go next – to try out the idea.

Alternatively, the teacher could draw on the story of Sinon the Greek in *The Odyssey* and say in role: 'I seek a volunteer, a fearless cunning person, I seek someone who is brave enough to be able to pretend that they have deserted from the Greek army; someone brave enough to go to the Trojans and give themselves up. And cunning enough to be able to convince the Trojans that the giant wooden horse has been made as a gift for the gods to ensure our safe voyage home, cunning enough to be able to convince the Trojans that we made the horse as big as it is because we wanted it to be impossible for them to take it into their city.'

Having chosen the person to deceive the Trojans, making the selection significant, using techniques similar to those used to find the person to negotiate with Achilles, 'We need to work together to help prepare this person for the task.'

> In *The Aeneid* and *The Odyssey*, the Greek who tricked the Trojans was named Sinon. For the sake of brevity that is how I shall refer to the character here.

The preparations of Sinon again involve collective speech writing, demanding discussions of the content of the speech, the order in which things are said, the kind of words, vocabulary and tone.

To ensure that Sinon is properly prepared for the delivery of the speech, we might use Forum Theatre for some practice sessions. Another way of preparing the speech maker for the encounter with the Trojans would be for the class to divide into pairs and for everyone to try the speech out; their findings reported back and fed into improving the speech.

> The speech making can thus become part of the fictional world, with the protection it offers. It is also a fine example of writing for purpose and exemplifies to the class the usefulness of redrafting.

Sinon the Greek delivers the prepared speech to the Trojans.

> The preparations for this moment all serve to increase the dramatic tension in advance of the interaction between Sinon and the Trojans. The class, however, have been alternating roles between Greeks and Trojans. Out of role, they know that Sinon is a spy. My inclination at this point would be to use the form adopted for the earlier exchanges involving speeches, with the teacher in role as the Trojan meeting Sinon, using Forum Theatre to enable you to consult the class and ask their advice about how to respond to the speech. Taking on that role also enables you to use the exchange to refer to specific contributions made by children in their work on making the giant horse: 'I see you have made the mane and the tail of your horse from the hair of your slain warriors.' You might be sceptical about the horse until you notice a small and telling detail, 'Greeks would never ... if they intended to trick us,' deliberately selecting the work of children whose confidence needs boosting.

Part 4 The Wooden Horse

In role, teacher reflects on Sinon's speech and the responses to it amongst the Trojans. 'How are we to take the horse into our great city? It is too big to take through the gates.'

Trojans taking the horse in. Trojan children looking at the horse. What they tell their friends. Pairs or small group improvisations.

Image theatre – a range of attitudes to the horse.

Inside the horse

As the Greek warriors wait for Sinon to release them, what are they thinking? Describe the conditions.

Discussion out of role

What do the Greek warriors intend to do when they are released from the horse? If the class knows the stories of the Fall of Troy, this will inform the discussion.

The dangers of trying to dramatise the destruction of Troy is that it could unleash chaos, affirming the negative stereotypes of boys as violent and insensitive. If tackled with care, however, it has the potential to enrich the drama and provide deep learning opportunities. The key is to seek ways of *slowing the drama down*, enabling us to dwell on moments, to explore the significance of the violence rather than trivialising it. Edward Bond's concept of 'accident time' is pertinent in this context. (See p35)

In small groups, prepare a scene to be enacted in slow motion, lasting ten seconds, showing one act of violence somewhere in the city. Important constraint: no actual physical contact to take place between group members. Groups have to find a way of representing the violence, killing, destruction through slow motion.

Using the ten second slow-motion killing, create five stop-motion or *still image* moments, along the lines of an *emotional map*.

Add one line for each stop motion moment for each side, ie Greeks and Trojans. What do you see, hear, smell? Focus on specifics and detail.

Active *storyboarding* in small groups: create a sequence of seven *still images* to show what happens when Sinon opens the hidden door to release the Greek warriors.

In role as a Homeric story teller, teacher summarises and reflects on the horror of the events – based on the storyboards of still images created by the groups. If the teacher can use heightened, formalised language in the narration, that enriches the class's experience and places their own work in a cultural context.

Part 5 Homecoming
Greeks returning home, having destroyed Troy

Teacher narrates:

'The Greeks had been away from their homes for ten years, there was not one of them who had not lost a close friend or relative in the battles. Now Troy has been taken, the great city destroyed. I wonder how those brave warriors feel now? I wonder what they see as they look back at what remains of the city?'

Poetic montage

Using a selection of one line extracts (see resources below), groups (or individuals) create a five line poem to give an impression of the destruction of Troy glimpsed and remembered by Greek raiders as they leave the burning city and start on their journey home.

Teacher asks the class to speak about one of the trophies they have taken from Troy and to tell where they found it; and then to describe one image of Troy that they will never forget, maybe starting by setting an example: 'I will never forget breaking into a room that I thought would be filled with treasure and finding nothing but a child crying.'

Small groups list the trophies they have taken from Troy.

> If you have used Part 2 of this material (*Inside the Walls of Troy*), the class will have made artefacts that can now become the trophies carried home by the Greeks. Because the groups will have made these and explored their significance for the Trojans, the objects will have rich contested meanings far beyond the literal.

Discussion
By taking part in the war against Troy

- what have they gained?
- what have they lost?
- what do they expect when they get home?
- what they will do with their trophies when they get home?

Image theatre

An image with the title 'Arriving Home'.

> The image should show the range of feelings of those returning and those awaiting their return. This could initially be created to look naturalistic – with others then joining the image and touching one of the participants to represent their inner feelings. The aim is to encourage the class to see the emotional complexity of the moment.

Forum Theatre, pair work or small group improvisations

The person returning home makes a gift of the stolen artefact to the person who has waited at home.

> It may be that by this stage in the project this scene can be played out 'cold'. Using Forum Theatre can protect the participants but, however the exchange is played out, it's important for the teacher to reflect on the significance of the object chosen as a gift. What meanings does each person imbue it with?

An alternative perspective

The drama presented in this chapter has focused on events in and near Troy. In Homer's *Odyssey*, Penelope is the wife of Odysseus. She waits twenty years for the final return of her husband. Time could also be spent considering the point of view of those left at home. How have they coped? What do they anticipate, expect, hope for, fear from the homecoming?

Part 6 Guardians of Troy

Modern day archaeologists asked to receive contemporary refugees

This part of the drama is set in the modern day. It draws on the earlier material, but recontextualises it, fictionalising an archaeological site of Troy.

This part of the project could be used as a way of reflecting on the earlier work and/or to develop aspects of it for performance; but it also further explores the concept of sanctuary, and relates the work on the Trojan War to the modern world.

In preparation for this work it would be useful for the class to look at photographs and plans of the real site – see resources below. It would be essential to introduce the work by stating clearly that it is fictional:

'Our drama is going to be set in 2008, at the archaeological remains of Troy. There is a real site where they have discovered a city very like the mythical Troy; but our site is part of our drama. We will need to work together to create it.' When the children have understood that concept of the imagined site,

166

then the teacher moves into role, using Mantle of the Expert. The class are cast as archaeologists at the World Heritage Site of ancient Troy.

Their responsibilities are:

- to ensure the protection of the site
- to further understanding of the culture of the ancient city
- to make their findings accessible for a general public

In small groups, each takes responsibility for a particular area – geographical and/or topical – addressing such questions as: What is precious here? What specifically has to be protected? What can we allow to be seen by the general public? What has to be kept secret?

Using their experiences in earlier parts of the project, in small groups they recreate some of the rooms they explored as both Trojans and Greeks.

Writing in role

- inventory of items to go into an onsite museum
- floor plans of room(s) showing the difference between the ruin as it is now and the way they, the archaeologists, imagine it might have looked
- maps of the site – one for visitors, one for private use
- guide books
- reconstructions/video displays

The reconstructions give you a framework for taking aspects of the project towards performance. It is important to take time for the group to develop a strong commitment to the roles of archaeologists and to their responsibilities for the site itself. These responsibilities will shortly be challenged.

Teacher enters in role as a representative of International Refuge First, an organisation that aims to protect refugees from conflicts and natural disasters. The archaeological site is located near a war zone. It also has a plentiful natural water supply; and is an ideal location for setting up a refugee camp. IFR is evacuating a group of thirty refugees from a village that has been destroyed in the fighting. The description of the destruction of the village and the plight of the villagers could resonate strongly with the children's own work in Parts 4 and 5.

Negotiating for the use of the site.

Using the site for refugees.

Resources for use in *The Fall Of Troy*
Extracts for use in scenes, poems and speeches

Lines from The Iliad for use in Part 1 (developing dialogue in five scenes about the dead soldier)

It was no quarrel with the Trojan warriors that brought me here to fight .

You always enjoy predicting trouble.

The timbers of our ships have rotted.

Our wives and children sit at home and wait for us.

Use your eloquence to stop them.

A leader who grows fat on his own people.

He will not like to hear it. He is difficult .

My quarrel is not with you.

Oh Lord Apollo hear my prayer. Lord put my pain to sleep.

He knows nothing of the disaster affecting the army.

You never have the courage to go into battle with the men.

It will get worse.

Save your hate. It will keep.

Why is he so concerned about a few casualties?

This flesh is mine. I got him first.

Be quiet now .

I have pined and wept.

Was all that life a dream?

Don't make your son an orphan and your wife a widow.

Don't distress yourself. War is men's business.

Take a deep breath before you speak.

We did not want to come to Troy.

We could not disobey our father's words.

Are you ready to fight?

Are you willing to die?

Starting point of Odysseus's speech to the Greek soldiers on the shore of Troy

To be completed ....

I know this hardship is wearying to everyone,

I understand the urge to go.

Just one month at sea, far from his family,

will make a raider sick of the rowing bench,

sick of his ship, as gales and rising seas

delay him even a month!

As for ourselves,

now is the ninth year that we keep the siege.

I cannot blame you men for sickening

here on the Trojan shore.

But it would shame us all to stay so long

and sail home empty handed.

Hold on, dear friends!

Extracts for use in completing Odysseus's speech to the Greek soldiers

Put down your arms, run to your ships, launch them by dark.

We are Greeks. We fight to win.

If one is lost, close his eyes, step over him, and kill his enemy.

To waste our king's dream is to scorn our dead

Take Troy by total war. Then sail safe home.

Never forget that we are born to kill.

Hold back the night until I break into Hector's body with my spear.

Lead on, brave king, as you have led before, and we shall follow.

All the above extracts are edited and adapted from *The Iliad,* translated by Robert Fitzgerald (1974)

Extracts for use in Part 5 – Homecoming

Note – The first four of the following lines are from Virgil's *The Aeneid* (trans. John Dryden), the remainder are adapted from *The Iliad.*

> The sacred altars, from whose flames we fled
>
> Houses and holy temples floating in blood
>
> Troy's lofty towers in ashes lay
>
> her stolen statues
>
> broad city
>
> lofty gates
>
> fine towers
>
> wide streets
>
> a spear stuck in the sand
>
> the light of evening has begun
>
> It leaves me cold
>
> Look back to the ridge that is empty now
>
> a thousand fires
>
> a million footprints
>
> Troy silent
>
> broken walls sullen beneath the smoke
>
> too young to die
>
> I need forgiveness too

Further resources

The Iliad is available in numerous versions. A good literal translation is available in a Penguin Classics edition: *The Iliad,* translated by E.V. Rieu

Modern retellings and reworkings of *The Iliad*

Rosemary Sutcliffe (1993) *Black Ships Before Troy*
Winner of the Kate Greenaway Medal. Beautifully written and illustrated. Highly recommended.

James Reeves (1968) *The Trojan Horse*
Reeves was a fine poet and children's author in his own right. This is a condensed poetic modern retelling for young people.

Peter Connolly (1998) *The Ancient Greece of Odysseus*
A straightforward retelling of *The Iliad* and *The Odyssey*, with vivid illustrations, and reliable historical information about the world of Troy and the Ancient Greeks.

Christopher Logue's *War Music* is not aimed at children. It is a powerful adaptation or 'an account' as Logue calls it. Some extracts have been used in the project. (See bibliography for publication details).

War Music
All Day Permanent Red (the first battle scenes)
Cold Calls

War with Troy: The Story of Achilles – three CD audio retelling of the Trojan War, created for children in upper primary and lower secondary, particularly aimed at developing speaking, listening and literacy skills. The CDs are divided into twelve episodes of about 15 minutes each. Published by Cambridge School Classics Project.

In Search of the Trojan War, Michael Wood, BBC Books, 2005 (revised paperback edition). For teachers – an excellent, very accessible account of the discovery and archaeological excavations of Troy, and an investigation into the truth behind Homer's poems and the associated legends. The associated six part BBC series is available on DVD.

Websites
Cambridge School Classics Project:
http://www.cambridgescp.com/main_entrance.php

History of the Trojan War – a brief, accessible account.
http://www.stanford.edu/~plomio/history.html

Reconstructions of Ancient Troy can be found at:
http://www.uni-tuebingen.de/troia/vr/vr0207_en.html

Refugees International website
www.refugeesinternational.org

Glossary of drama techniques

Whilst I recognise that many people using this book will be familiar with the terms used in these projects, I hope there will also be readers who are new to educational drama. I offer the following glossary to describe some of the techniques that are referred to in the projects. It is necessarily brief. There are many good books in which the techniques are discussed in depth.

I consciously refer to them as techniques and not 'strategies' or 'conventions', as they are sometimes described. They are tools to enable you to explore situations, to ensure that as many children as possible have a stake in the drama, that everyone's voice is heard. It's important not to let them take over and become the raison d'être of the drama.

All of the techniques described here serve to *slow down the drama*, enabling you to encourage reflection, to tease out meaning, to focus on detail.

Conscience alley

Someone facing a dilemma in a drama walks slowly between two lines formed by the group. As they pass each person, those on one side comment aloud in support of a course of action whilst those on the other side give reasons against it. At the end of the alley, the character has to make a decision based on what they have heard. The technique is similar to Forum Theatre in that it gives every member of the group a chance to participate. As with all these techniques, it is easily adapted – for example, those on one side of the alley voice hopes, while the other side voice fears.

Emotional map

A map marking not geographical locations and spatial relationships, but emotional staging points; a way of reflecting on personal journeys.

Forum Theatre

The technique was developed by Augusto Boal, a South American theatre director, inspired by the work of the educationalist, Paulo Freire. It has been much adapted by drama teachers. At its simplest, a dramatic exchange (involving a small number of people) is played out in front of the whole group. The group has the power to stop the drama at any point and suggest alternative directions which it might take, or volunteer to take over a role for a re-run of the action. In this book it is often used as a kind of collaborative playwriting, and I use the idea of the Forum as a kind of market place, where ideas are exchanged. Constructing the teacher in role as a character in a drama thus becomes a kind of Forum Theatre. *The Pet Cellar* and *The Arrival* include accounts of the technique in use. Towards the end of *The Arrival* project, Forum Theatre is used in a way closer to Boal's.

Image Theatre

Another technique developed by Augusto Boal, described in detail in his book *Games for Actors and Non-Actors*. Essentially this involves a small group making a *still image* or sequence of images. As soon as the group have been given the title, they try to make the image – but without any talking amongst themselves – within a given short time limit. When the time is up, they have to freeze whether they feel they have achieved the task or not. One person then steps outside the image, looks at it carefully and models all the participants as if they were clay or plasticine. When satisfied, s/he steps back into the image. Then the next person steps out and does the same. Each person can change the image as much or as little as they like – but they must not return the image to the way it has been before. When every person in the group is satisfied with the image, it is complete. The exercise encourages non-verbal communication and co-operation (Boal 1992: 164-5).

Mantle of the Expert

This 'denotes that moment when the teacher deliberately reverses the usual teacher/pupil relationship and bestows expertise on the children.' (Havell 1987: 174) Discussed in detail in the chapter *Dramatic Writing and Process Drama*.

Marking the moment

A means of encouraging reflection on the drama work. Students recall a particular place or moment in the drama which was significant to them. This can be done through out-of-role discussion or, in role, through a piece of action or still image. Relates to the idea of an *emotional map*. Can also be used at an early stage in moving towards performance.

Role on the wall

Provides a visual aid for developing thinking about character(s), a means of recording information about characters in graphic form. Discussed in detail in *Character and Role*. See pp29-31.

Still images/freeze frame

Groups or individuals use their bodies to create a three dimensional image of a given moment, as if that moment had been freeze framed on a video or DVD. Can be used to focus on body language and facial expressions; as a way of moving from comic strip or storyboard images to improvisations. Useful in conjunction with *thought tracking*.

Thought tracking

Pupils, other than those playing a role, are given an opportunity to say what they think the thoughts and feelings of characters in role might be. Can be added to *still images/freeze frames* or become part of a *Forum Theatre* – for example, what might she be thinking at this point? *Conscience alley* is one way of formalising thought tracking.

Twilighting

Sometimes it is useful to move into a drama gradually, to prepare the ground, to spend some time in the *twilight* zone between reality and the drama. Examples can be found at the beginning of *The Kraken*, where the children make fantasy creatures; at the beginning of *The Arrival*, where they look at an illustration; and the small group tasks suggested as preparatory work before *The Fall of Troy*.

SECTION FOUR

Resources

Playwriting – guidelines

- play writing can be thought of as an extension of writing in role; an activity which has the potential to stimulate, to motivate and to liberate children's writing, which provides opportunities for children to write for purpose and to learn from their participation in drama through reflection

- play writing enables children to experiment with a wide range of voices in order to find that which is most appropriate in any given context. It encourages close attention to: rhythm of language, choice of vocabulary, register, tone

- play writing can be woven into the fiction of a developing process drama, can be used at the end of a process drama as a way of re-flecting on it and then sharing the work with others

- working within tight constraints is more of a stimulus to the imagina-tion than a brake on it. Tackling manageable 'tasks' helps avoid writ-ing blocks and draws attention to the processes of dramatic writing. Always encourage children to *use* the given constraints rather than to break or undermine them

- all writing should be seen as *work in progress*. All writers, be they published novelists and playwrights or young children struggling with their first words on paper, learn from the processes they under-take

- drama is a social and collaborative art form. Good drama and good dramatic writing encourages close accurate observation – of others, of social situations and of ourselves in social contexts

■ it is as important to find ways of reflecting on writing and developing it through reflection as it is to find ways of liberating the imagination. Redrafting work as a result of processes of reflection can be as creative as any other part of the process

■ there is no single correct way of developing skills and expertise as a dramatic writer. What we can do is to suggest tasks, activities, patterns and methods of work that can enable individuals to develop their own skills

■ just as there is no correct way of writing, plays themselves can take on numerous forms. When developing playwriting skills with young people, it is worth developing short self-contained plays, thinking about conciseness, structure and dialogue. Economy of expression is a skill in its own right. Very short plays can be remarkably provocative and stimulating

Photocopiable Materials

Here you will find a range of material that can be photocopied and used with children.

Dialogue extracts

Jack and the Beanstalk

What shall we do? What shall we do?
Cheer up, mother.

I'll get work somewhere.
Nobody will take you.

We'll have to sell the cow.
Oh no.

We'll use the money to open a shop.
All right, mother. It's market day today.

Good morning, Jack.
Good morning to you.

And where are you off to?
I'm going to market to sell our cow.

Two in each hand and one in your mouth.
And here they are, the very beans themselves.

Your cow for these beans.
You've got to be joking.

If it's not true, you can have your cow back.
Right.

I'm home.
Back already, Jack?

How much did you get for the cow?
You'll never guess.

They're magic beans.
Go to your room.

Could you be so kind as to give me breakfast?
It's breakfast you'll be if you don't run off.

Come on quick. Jump in here.
In there?

Dialogue extracts
Starting points for short plays

The extracts for older children are attributed to A and B. This demands a conceptual leap. When using the exercise with younger children, you might attribute the dialogue to faces.

The following can be used as starting points for developing short plays, to speculate about the story or play from which they are taken, the order in which scenes appear, what the book might be about, its characters and concerns (as in the chapter on *Wolves in the Walls*); or used within a fiction as part of a process drama (as in *The Arrival*).

A You're not allowed to wear that.
B Who says?

A When was that?
B Not telling.

A Can I? Now?
B Show me what you've done so far.

A Eat up for mummy.
B Don't want to.

A Have you got the right money?
B Here. That's all I got.

A What do you say? I asked you. What do you say?
B Sorry.

A I told you we shouldn't.
B You always say that.

A Ten.
B I don't believe you.

A Can you see them?
B: See what?

A: What was I doing?
B: Smiling.

A Sugar's not fattening. I know it's not fattening. I know.
B Who says?

A It's only till tomorrow.
B But Dad ...

A Alright then, just this once.
B I'll pay you back. I promise.

A She made me do it.
B She wasn't even in the room.

A Can we go swimming after?
B Don't speak with your mouth full.

A I've swapped it.
B Mum'll murder you.

A We've got three computers at home.
B We've even got one in the toilet.

The following extracts are from *Dirty Rascals* by Paul Swift.

A My dad's shop sells everything.
B I bet it doesn't.

A You shouldn't play in here.
B Why not?

A Where's my tea?
B I can't do everything at once, can I?

A I'll stick up for you.
B Will you, really?

A You can't be a gasman.
B I can if I want.

A Do you want to play something?
B Yeah, alright. School.

A Who's boss?
B Me cos I'm the cleverest.

A We've all got to tell a secret.
B You first.

A When I grow up I'm going to be rich.
B But what are you going to do?

A What have you got there?
B It's my secret stone. It's got magic powers

Swift (1987)

Missing lines (Exercise on p24)

What are you doing?
wasn't yesterday
think we're lost

Dave come with us
kidding me
push me

you should sit down
forty five
I don't believe you

something to eat
wanted to help
raining

nothing to hide
well good
if you like

One line matches for matching dialogue exercise

These have been grouped into:

A – beginners (questions)
B – beginners (responses)

A – middling
B – middling

A – difficult (non sequiturs)
B – difficult (non-sequiturs)

There are ten lines in each group. There is no reason why two or more children in each group could not be given the same line. The subsequent discussions could be very productive.

A LINES (beginners – questions)

Should you play in there?

Where do you live?

Will you stick up for me?

Do you know everything?

Do you want to play something?

Shall I show you something?

What have you got there?

Can you keep a secret?

Are you going home now?

Can I come with you?

B LINES (beginners – responses)

Why not?

I can if I want.

Might do.

So what if I do?

It's a secret.

Sometimes.

Depends.

What?

I don't know.

Who've you been talking to?

A LINES (middling)

When I grow up I'm going to be rich.

I feel sorry for him.

Just sit still and it might go away.

If you ask me, he had it coming.

I think it's for you.

I hate Sundays.

We live over the shop.

This one looks interesting.

Are you sure he's asleep?

We've all got to tell a secret.

B LINES (middling)

Yeah, but how?

I think he had a late night.

You just have to make an effort.

I think we should get a doctor.

Do you really expect me to believe that?

I hate Mondays.

Yes, but we've still got to pay for it.

Looks aren't everything.

That's not fair.

I think we should phone the police.

A Lines (difficult)

I can't do everything at once, can I?

It's much too heavy to take on holiday.

You'll just have to make an effort.

Do you want to play something?

It's time you got your hair cut.

What are you doing Saturday afternoon?

It's your turn to do the washing up.

I know someone keeps a snake in the fish tank.

Maybe we should try Euro Disney for a change.

Mum says you shouldn't have pets at Christmas.

B Lines (difficult)

I won't be able to drive.

That's not fair.

Just suppose he did.

I can't do everything at once, can I?

Do you want to go down to the shop?

Did you see East Enders last night?

I should see a doctor if I were you.

When was that then?

Not now. I'm busy.

But what are you going to do?

Blank five image storyboard

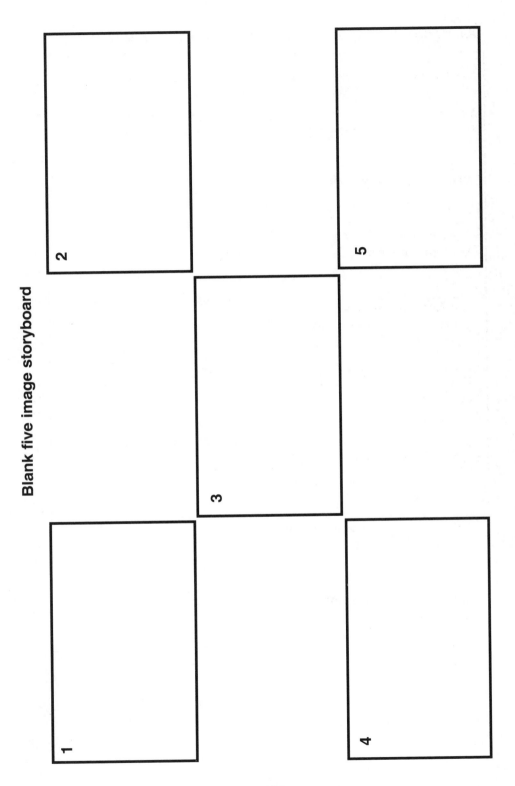

Observing people questionnaires (See Chapter 5 in Section 2)

Thinking of a real person you have often seen, but never actually spoken to, answer the following:

OBSERVED BEHAVIOUR

Three short statements of fact	
A possession or item of clothing that you associate with this person	
A sound that you associate with this person – but not something s/he says	
Something you *have* heard this person say	
The time of day when you have most often seen this person	
An object or item of furniture that you might associate with this person	
ADDITIONAL INFORMATION/ QUESTIONS	

What you imagine about this person, based on what you have observed

Something that you *imagine* this person really wants to do in his/her life; something that drives them	
Could be rephrased as 'What do you *imagine* might make this person really happy?	
A fear that this person might be willing to admit to other people	
A fear that s/he is *not* willing to admit to other people	
Something you might *imagine* someone else saying *to* this person ...	
Who says this?	
And what do you imagine the person you have observed replies?	
And *where* does this happen?	

The observation questionnaire adapted for use with a fictional character from a book (See example at end of *Wolves in the Walls* chapter)

Question	Responses
The name of the person you want to write about in your play	
A possession or item of clothing that you associate with this person	
Three short statements about him or her based on what you know from the book	
A sound that you associate with this person – but not something s/he says	
Something s/he says	
A time of day	
An object or item of furniture that you might associate with this person	
What does s/he want?	
A fear that s/he *is* willing to admit to other people	
A fear that s/he is *not* willing to admit to other people	

Imagine this person talking to someone s/he doesn't speak to in the book

Who is s/he talking to?	
Where are they talking?	
Something you might *imagine* this person saying, that she *doesn't* actually say in the book	
And what does the other person reply?	

Other Resources

Recommended books

Full bibliographic information appears in the Bibliography (p197).

Baldwin, P (2004) *With Drama in Mind: Real Learning in Imagined Worlds*

Baldwin, P and Fleming, K (2003) *Teaching Literacy Through Drama*
'Designed to help teachers meet National Curriculum and National Literacy Strategy requirements through the integration of speaking, listening, reading and writing.'

Boal, Augusto, *Theatre of the Oppressed*
This is the book where Boal first proposed his ideas for Forum Theatre. The book places this in a theatrical context, relating it to the theories of Aristotle and Brecht.

Boal, Augusto, *Games for Actors and Non Actors*
The book contains further work on Forum Theatre. Although there is some theoretical underpinning, this is more of a handbook of ideas and exercises than *Theatre of the Oppressed*. There is much in here about Image Theatre.

Bolton, G (1998) *Acting in Classroom Drama: A Critical Analysis*

Fines, John and Verrier, Ray (1974) *The Drama of History*
This is now sadly out of print, but it remains an excellent book. An obituary to John Fines can be found in Online Resources p195.

Heathcote, D and Bolton, G (1995) *Drama for Learning: Dorothy Heathcote's Mantle of the Expert Approach to Education*
A collection of illuminating essays by Dorothy Heathcote and Gavin Bolton, edited by Cecily O'Neill

Morgan, N and Saxton, J (1987) *Teaching Drama*
A very practical book. Thorough and detailed. Particularly useful on teaching in role and questioning strategies for teachers

O'Neill, C (1995) *Drama Worlds: A framework for process drama*

Taylor, P and Warner, C (eds) (2006) *Structure and Spontaneity: the process drama of Cecily O'Neil*

Wagner, B-J (1979) *Dorothy Heathcote: Drama As a Learning Medium*
The first book to discuss Dorothy Heathcote's innovative methods and pedagogy. A great deal of excellent practice described in this book. Particularly useful for its chapters on planning and working in-role. Now republished in a revised edition by Trentham.

Woolland, B (2009) *Drama in the Primary School*
Extensively revised and updated edition of *The Teaching of Drama in the Primary School* (first published 1993).

Winston, J (2004) *Drama and English at the Heart of the Primary Curriculum*

Winston, J (2000) *Drama, Literacy and Moral Education 5-11*

Playwriting and creative writing

There are several books about playwriting but, to my knowledge, there is nothing specifically aimed at the primary school age range. The following might, however, be useful to teachers able to adapt ideas:

Greig, Noel (2004) *Playwriting: A Practical Guide*
Noel Greig has run numerous workshops on playwriting 'in a wide range of communities and contexts', including Primary and Secondary Schools. The book contains well over a hundred different exercises, all of which can be adapted.

An excellent book, thoroughly recommended.

Hughes, Ted (1967) *Poetry in the Making*
First published in 1967, this is still an inspirational book. Based on a series of programmes that Hughes wrote for BBC Schools, it was intended for use as a text and an anthology for use in class or as a handbook for teachers and writers. Although the book makes no references to plays as such, it contains excellent advice – especially about the importance of close observation and attention to detail. There is much material here that could be used with children in upper Primary.

Redington C (ed) (1987) *Six Theatre in Education Programmes*
This includes the play, *Dirty Rascals* by Paul Swift, from which some of the dialogue extracts are taken.

Film, Television and DVD material

The British Film Institute has developed an excellent teaching guide to using film and television with 3 to 11-year-olds, entitled *Look Again!* It outlines the close connections between teaching literacy and cineliteracy, and shows how to integrate these activities across the curriculum in Primary Schools. The *BFI* also produces *Starting Stories* for Primary Schools. (See *BFI* website opposite).

Film Education offers a wealth of free educational materials, resources and services which have been developed in response to the growing importance of Media Education in the National Curriculum.

Film: 21st Century Literacy aims to 'help children and young people to use, enjoy and understand moving images; not just to be technically capable but to be culturally literate too...'

Online resources and Internet links

Drama in education

Dorothy Heathcote Archive
http://www.partnership.mmu.ac.uk/dha/

John Fines – obituary in *International Journal of Historical Learning, Teaching and Research* Volume 2, Number 2 July 2002
www.centres.ex.ac.uk/historyresource/journal4/LTPSPEAK.doc

London Drama
http://www.londondrama.org/

Mantle of the Expert
http://www.mantleoftheexpert.com/index.php

Bealings School Mantle of the Expert projects
http://www.bealings.org.uk/exciting-projects/mantle-of-the-expert/

NATD, the National Association for the Teaching of Drama
http://www.natd.net/

National Drama
http://www.nationaldrama.co.uk/

Film

British Film Institute resources for Primary Schools
http://www.bfi.org.uk/education/teaching/primary.html

Film Education
http://www.filmeducation.org/

Film: 21st Century Literacy
http://21stcenturyliteracy.org.uk/

National Curriculum and Arts Council documentation

Drama in schools (Arts Council England document)
http://www.artscouncil.org.uk/documents/publications/725.pdf

National Curriculum Creativity documentation:
http://curriculum.qca.org.uk/key-stages-1-and-2/learning-across-the-curriculum/creativity/index.aspx

Primary Framework for literacy and mathematics
http://www.standards.dfes.gov.uk/primaryframework/literacy/

Theatre and Theatre in Education

Applied and Interactive Theatre Guide
http://www.tonisant.com/aitg/

Big Brum Theatre in Education Company
http://www.bigbrum.org.uk/

National Theatre website. *The National Theatre* has an active Education Department. Their *Primary Shakespeare Project* focuses on literacy, oracy, creative writing, drama, music, design and movement for Year 5 and Year 6 classes and their teachers.
http://www.nationaltheatre.org.uk/education

University of Exeter has a webpage which gives links to most UK Theatre in Education companies: http://spa.ex.ac.uk/drama/links/theatreedu.html

Bibliography

Baldwin, P (2004) *With Drama in Mind: Real Learning in Imagined Worlds.* Edinburgh: Network Educational Press

Baldwin, P and Fleming, K (2003) *Teaching Literacy Through Drama.* London: Routledge Falmer

Boal, A (1992) *Games for Actors and Non Actors.* London: Routledge

Boal, A (1979) *Theatre of the Oppressed.* London: Pluto

Bragg, M (1986) *The Pet Cellar.* London: Methuen Children's Books

Brecht, B (1935) (trans. Willett, J) 'The Playwright's Song'. In Willett, J (ed) (1995) *Bad Time for Poetry – 152 Poems and Songs.* London: Methuen

Brecht, B (1964) (trans. Willett, J) *Brecht on Theatre.* London: Methuen

Bolton, G (1998) *Acting in Classroom Drama: a Critical Analysis.* Stoke on Trent: Trentham

Bond, E (1999) *The Hidden Plot: Notes on Theatre and the State.* London: Methuen.

Bowell, P and Heap, B (2001) *Planning Process Drama.* London: Falmer

Browne, A (1998) *Voices in the Park.* London: Doubleday

Davies, G (1983) *Practical Primary Drama.* London: Heinemann

Davis, D (ed) 2005 *Edward Bond and the Dramatic Child.* Stoke on Trent: Trentham

Fines, J (1994) 'Evidence: the basis of the discipline.' In H Bourdillon (ed) *Teaching History.* London: Routledge

Fines, J and Verrier, V (1974) *The Drama of History.* London: Clive Bingley

Foakes, R (1993) *Hamlet versus Lear: Cultural Politics and Shakespeare's Art.* Cambridge: Cambridge University Press

Freire, P (1970) *Pedagogy of the Oppressed.* London: Penguin Books

Gaiman, G and Mckean, D (2003) *The Wolves in the Walls.* London: Bloomsbury

Goffman, E (1969) *The Presentation of Self in Everyday Life.* Harmondsworth: Allen Lane, The Penguin Press

Greig, N (2005) *Playwriting.* London: Routledge

Hampshire Inspection and Advisory Service (2005) *Primary Drama Handbook.* Winchester: Hampshire County Council

Havell, C (1987) 'A Reconstruction of the Development of Drama in Education.' In P Abbs (ed) *Living Powers.* Lewes: Falmer Press

Heathcote, D and Bolton, G (1995) *Drama for Learning: Dorothy Heathcote's Mantle of the Expert Approach to Education.* Portsmouth, NH: Heinemann

Homer, trans Rieu, E (1950) *The Iliad.* Harmondsworth: Penguin

Homer, trans Fitzgerald, R (1974) *The Iliad.* Oxford: Oxford University Press

Hughes, T (1967) *Poetry in the Making.* London: Faber and Faber

Hulson, M (2006) *Schemes for Classroom Drama.* Stoke on Trent: Trentham

Lacey, S and Woolland, B (1992) Educational Drama and Radical Theatre Practice. *New Theatre Quarterly* Vol VIII No 29, February 1992 p81-91

Logue, C (2005) *Cold Calls.* London: Faber and Faber

Logue, C (2003) *All Day Permanent Red.* London: Faber and Faber

Logue, C (2001) *War Music.* London: Faber and Faber

McEntagart, T (1981) Play and Theatre. *SCYPT Journal* No 7

McKee, D (1980) *Not Now Bernard.* London: Andersen Press

Morgan, N and Saxton, J (1987) *Teaching Drama.* London: Hutchinson.

Nichol, J (2002) John Fines 1938-1999. *International Journal of Historical Learning, Teaching and Research* Vol 2, No 2 July 2002

O'Neill, C (1995) *Drama Worlds: A framework for process drama.* Portsmouth, New Hampshire: Heinemann

O'Neill, C and Lambert, A (1982) *Drama Structures: A practical handbook for teachers.* Cheltenham: Stanley Thornes

Prévert, J., trans Ferlinghetti, L (1965) *Paroles.* Harmondsworth: Penguin

Swift, P (1987) Dirty Rascals. In C. Redington (ed) *Six Theatre in Education Programmes.* London: Methuen

Shor, I and Freire, P (1987) *A Pedagogy of Liberation: Dialogues on Transforming Education.* South Hadley, MA: Bergin and Garvey.

Tan, S (2006) *The Arrival.* New York: Arthur A. Levine Books

Taylor, P and Warner, C (eds) (2006) *Structure and Spontaneity: the process drama of Cecily O'Neill.* Stoke on Trent: Trentham

Vygotsky, L (1978) *Mind in Society: Development of Higher Psychological Processes.* Cambridge, MA: Harvard University Press

Wagner, B-J (1979) *Dorothy Heathcote: Drama As a Learning Medium.* London: Hutchinson

Wallis, M and Shepherd, S (1998) *Studying Plays.* London: Arnold

Wiles, D (2000) *Greek Theatre Performance – an Introduction.* Cambridge: Cambridge University Press

Winston, J (2004) *Drama and English at the Heart of the Primary Curriculum.* London: David Fulton

Winston, J (2000) *Drama, Literacy and Moral Education 5-11.* London: David Fulton

Woolland, B (1993) *The Teaching of Drama in the Primary School.* Harlow: Longman

Woolland, B (2009) *Drama in the Primary School.* Harlow: Pearson

Index

accident time 35, 164
audience 6, 9, 10, 18, 20, 32, 35, 38, 46-47, 51, 92, 106, 123, 142

Big Brum Theatre in Education Company 196
Boal, Augusto 11, 174, 193
    see also Forum Theatre
Bolton, Gavin 12, 34, 193
Bond, Edward 35, 55, 164, 197
Brecht, Bertholt 32, 38, 55, 136, 193, 197
British Film Institute (*bfi*) 48, 194
Browne, Anthony 50, 85-89

change
    drama and change 11, 36-38, 50
    structure and change 39-40
character
    character and role 27-34
    character construction 17, 19, 28, 31-32, 56, 65, 81-82, 98, 137, 158, 174
Chekhov, Anton 32
collaborative play making 6, 9, 54, 95, 155-156
collaborative speech writing
    see speech writing
conscience alley 173, 175
creativity 3-4, 50, 133, 196

Davis, David 7, 12, 35, 197
dialogue 6, 10, 17-26, 31, 33, 35-36, 39, 43-44, 61
    see also each of the practical projects
dialogue exercises
    camouflaging dialogue 19-22, 43, 106, 150
    missing lines 24, 184
    one line matches 23, 185-188
Drama in schools 196
dramatic frame 43, 46, 130, 132-133
dramatic irony 34

film 39, 92, 129, 194, 195
Fines, John vii, 1, 12, 13, 193, 195, 197
Forum Theatre 11, 19, 31-2, 64, 65, 67, 70, 76, 81-82, 107, 108, 121, 122, 125, 140, 142, 145, 157, 160, 166, 173, 174, 175, 193
freeze frame see still image
Freire, Paulo 4, 5, 174

Greig, Noel 17, 29, 38, 40, 194, 197

Heathcote, Dorothy 12, 13, 34, 64, 96, 193, 195, 197, 198
Homer 45, 153, 161, 166, 176, 197
Homeric storyteller (role of) 165
Hulson, Maggie 151, 198

Iliad, The 54, 153, 156-8, 159, 161
lines from for speech writing 168-170
image theatre 174, 193
imagination 27, 30, 55-56, 58-59, 106, 160, 177, 178
language, figurative 51-52, 54, 106
literacy 3-4, 6, 7, 8, 17, 19, 21, 29, 46, 52, 63, 69-71, 82-83, 102, 113, 145-147, 171, 193, 194
Little Red Riding Hood 30, 46
Logue, Christopher 155, 171, 198
London Drama 195

Mantle of the Expert 13, 14, 64, 76,161-162, 167, 174, 193, 195, 197
maps 12, 42-43, 68, 70, 82, 96, 102, 108, 140, 147, 155, 167
    emotional 43, 54, 70, 108, 156
marking the moment 174
McEntagart, Tag 95, 198
meaning beyond the literal 49-54 see also metonym, metaphor, symbol(ism)
metaphor 35, 49-53, 75, 94-95, 112, 123
metonym 51-52
missing lines exercise 24, 184

narrative 9, 35-48, 66, 71, 77-78, 81, 91, 94, 97, 99, 106, 108, 137, 150, 157
narrator, teacher as 48, 68, 99-100, 136, 137-138, 140, 141, 157, 160, 161, 165
National Association for the Teaching of Drama (NATD) 195
National Curriculum 3-4, 8, 39, 91, 99, 194, 196 see also Primary Framework
National Theatre 196
National Theatre of Scotland 108

O' Neill, Cecily 9, 12, 14, 34, 193, 198
observation 31, 55-61, 75, 177, 194
observing people questionnaire 58-61, 110, 190-192
Odysseus 45, 153, 154, 157-158, 166
Odyssey, The 153, 161, 162, 163, 170
online resources 72, 108, 151, 171, 195-196

photocopiable materials 179-192
Pied Piper of Hamelin 46
planning 63, 79, 87, 129-133, 154, 193
playwright 1-3, 9, 10, 17, 28-29, 32, 51, 55, 150
teacher as 47
playwright, skills and craft of 6, 17, 56
Primary Framework for literacy and mathematics 3, 196
Primary Shakespeare Project 196

process drama 5-6, 9-14, 17, 18, 19, 25-26, 27-28, 32-4, 46-48, 124, 177, 183, 198 see also practical projects: The Kraken, The Arrival, The Fall of Troy.
reading in role 15, 47, 53, 83, 96, 97
redrafting 163, 178
reflection 6, 9, 10, 42, 48, 52, 95, 106, 148, 160, 173, 174, 177, 178
refugees 153, 166-167, 171
rhythm 6, 11, 18, 20, 21, 33, 43-44, 47, 177
role see character and role, reading in role, teaching in role, writing in role
role on the wall 29, 69, 108, 175

scripts 25, 39, 150
Shakespeare, William 32, 49-50
speech writing, collaborative 144, 150, 157-158, 160, 163
resources for use in 169, 170
Stanislavski, C. 32
stereotypes 32, 164
still image 31, 39, 68, 69, 71, 87, 89, 92, 108, 123, 124-125, 134, 136, 140, 149, 156, 164, 174, 175
storyboards 39-40, 41, 42, 44, 48, 68, 69, 82, 89, 106-107, 108, 129, 148, 149, 150, 164, 175
blank storyboard resource 189
structure 9-10, 33, 35-48, 81, 93, 97, 106, 123, 142, 178
symbol(ism) 51-53, 95, 101, 103 see also metaphor, meaning beyond the literal

teaching in role 14, 33-34, 37, 58, 65, 67, 76, 96-97, 143, 156, 159, 161, 163, 174, 193
television 44, 48, 59, 92, 194
Tempest, The 49, 51
thought tracking 175
twilighting 175

voice, concept of 11, 17-18, 20, 21, 81-82, 86-87, 89, 177 see also dialogue
Vygotsky, L.S. 5, 198

websites see online resources
wondering, as a teacher's skill to encourage reflection 10, 47, 57, 58, 93, 95, 97, 122, 134, 136, 138, 143, 165,
Wooden Horse, The 154, 161, 163, 164-165
writing for purpose 11, 25, 28, 163, 177
writing in role 5-6, 11-12, 17, 70-71, 73, 91, 96, 97, 125, 137, 138, 141, 143, 144, 145-147, 148, 150, 160, 162, 167, 177,